Format YOUR Print Book with Createspace*

*and Lulu, using Microsoft Word.

Format YOUR Print Book with Createspace*

TIM C. TAYLOR

*and Lulu, using Microsoft Word

ISBN-13:

978-1492892212

With thanks to Andrew Cyrus Hudson, who gave me permission to use his novel, *Drift*, for many of the screenshots. And for all those who took the time to tell me what they thought of the first edition!

Contents

PART 2 — A TYPICAL BOOK -CREATION WORKFLOW 45

One-page Summary: how to self-publish with Createspace........48

A typical Createspace workflow: DETAIL.................................49

Table of Figures

Word versions and screenshots in this book.

Screenshots are mostly taken from a mix of Word 2007, 2010 or 2013. For most topics in this book, each Word edition looks slightly different from the others, but the differences are only in minor cosmetic detail. Where there are more significant differences between editions, I have drawn attention to this in the text. Otherwise I have only shown screen images for one of the editions.

Introduction

A Proposition:

With nothing more than Microsoft Word and the knowledge contained in this book, you can create professional-looking paperbacks through Createspace and other print-on-demand suppliers.

Only a few years ago, the term *self-publishing* meant an author who couldn't get a deal with a proper publisher and so had his or her book printed either by a vanity publisher or by one of the print-on-demand suppliers. The result would be expensive, the printing and binding quality of the books would be awful, or both. eBooks were an afterthought that never sold.

Some of writing in those books was first class, but the paperback would look second rate.

Not any more!

I'm starting this book with a proposition: I believe it is possible to produce professional-looking paperbacks at Createspace (and other print-on-demand services) using nothing more than Microsoft Word (for Windows or Mac). If you want high quality images, you might need some additional software to manipulate images and produce the final PDF. In fact, I know this is true, because that's how I made the paperback edition of this book.

I've been using Microsoft Word since the very first edition, back in the 1980s when Word was only available on the Apple Mac, and I'll be showing you how to use Word 2003, 2007, 2010, and 2013. Although, Microsoft Word is the focus of this book, later on I'll take a look at some of the other tools that might tempt you such as the Adobe suite of Acrobat Pro, Photoshop, and InDesign.

A note for Mac users

In this book I will make reference to producing books using Word running on MacOS. However, I cannot claim to have produce books using Word for Mac, and the screenshots and text primarily reference Word for Windows.

For independent and self-published authors there's great emphasis at the moment on the importance of producing eBooks, and rightly so, because for most authors, the majority of your sales will be through eBooks. Yet printed books are still important. Reviews are vital to sell your eBooks, but many reviewers state that they will only review paperback copies. Goodreads giveaways are a useful tool but giveaways are currently only possible with paperbacks. A significant number of readers who purchase eBooks say that they are more likely to purchase an eBook if there is a corresponding paperback version, reasoning that if an author hasn't produced a paperback version then it's hardly a serious attempt at publication.

You need to impress your reviewers and writing a good book is not enough. You also need good cover art and a well-formatted book. If your book hasn't been formatted properly then reviewers will label you a time-wasting amateur before they've even begun to read your book.

Do yourself a favor and deliver a book that looks professional.

Although I will touch on wider issues (such as whether to use an ISBN from Createspace or use your own) this book is aimed at explaining how you can turn your book manuscript in Microsoft Word into a professionally laid out interior suitable for Createspace, Lulu, Lightning Source International, or one of the other POD suppliers.

Here's what I'll teach you:

1. Concepts you need to understand about book layout and typesetting. For example, which pages in your book should display a page header, and which must not.

2. Then I'll explain how to implement those typesetting concepts in Microsoft Word. I'll work primarily in the Windows version of Word 2007, 2010 and 2013, but I will also explain key differences in Word for Windows 2003, and Word for Mac 2008 & 2011. I've produced books using all of these Windows versions of Word, *but*

I have not used Word for Mac extensively and never to produce books. Users of other packages, such as InDesign or Open Office, will have to work a little harder, but most, if not all, of the techniques will translate to your package.

3. As we go along, I will give you tips on how to format your manuscript so you can quickly and safely switch from a print edition to eBook editions suitable for Amazon Kindle Direct Publishing and Smashwords. This isn't, however, a comprehensive guide to producing eBooks.

Who is Tim C. Taylor?

Who authored this book, and why should you listen to him?

For a start, I know Microsoft Word. We're old friends who have been working together for twenty-five years and counting. I spent twenty years working in the software industry where I used Word to produce technical documentation, legal contracts, procedure manuals, training materials, business analysis models... a wide variety of non-fiction. Some former colleagues might say there was some fiction in there too, but I really wouldn't pay them much attention!

I'm a science fiction author too, being traditionally published and recently self-published. I changed career to set up a publishing business, Greyhart Press, and to provide book design services. The dozens of paperback books and scores of eBooks I've produced range from spiritual guides heavy in images and call-out boxes through business 'how-to' guides, to a *New York Times* recommended book about the 2003 Iraq War by a photo-journalist who was there. I love working with first-time novelists to give them a good start and a quality looking book. I've produced works for more established writers too: Neil Gaiman, Stephen Baxter, Jeff Noon, Tanith Lee, Lauren Beukes, and Ian Watson spring to mind.

So I've plenty of experience in producing books, and a long career being paid to write teaching guides using Microsoft Word.

My hope is that in this book I can combine all those attributes to produce a book that will enable you to create the paperback book that your manuscript deserves.

Oh, and one last thing. I don't know about you, but I can't stand those books that say they're going to teach you something but turn out to be a series of hard sells to get you to buy the author's services. Well, in the interests of transparency, I do offer a paid book design service. However, you won't find a single advert for my services or recommendation to buy them. In fact, the reverse. The outcome I want most of all is for you to learn how to lay out your book for yourself so that you don't need to hire my services.

I mean that sincerely. Quite frankly, if you did try to hire me I would probably be forced to turn you away because I have more work than I can cope with.

However, I do run a website where I post updates to this book between editions, and if you ask a question about book formatting, I'll be delighted to answer you. You can find me at www.timctaylor.com

On my site, you can also find large color versions of the images in this book.

BEGIN HERE

Createspace is one of a number of PRINT-ON-DEMAND companies (Lulu and Lightning Source International are the other main players in this market). The idea is that you supply Createspace with a PDF or other file for the book's interior, and do the same for the cover (or use one of their templates). Once you're happy, you tell Createspace to print however many copies you want and then wait for them to be delivered to your door. The book will also be listed at places such as amazon.com for customers to purchase and have the book printed and delivered by Amazon without you getting involved at all (except to get paid!)

Simple!

There are plenty of places online that will give you a basic set of steps to follow that will explain how to use Createspace (see the section on where to find further information — [p242]). Chances are, they will ignore any mention of how to *format* the file you upload to Createspace. Unfortunately, that part is not simple, not unless you know what you're doing. Well, that's okay. That is why I wrote this book.

Throughout this book I will use an example manuscript from a commission I worked on, a book called *Drift*, by author Andrew Cyrus Hudson. *Drift* is a novel, and uses a standard fiction layout, although with a large page size. I chose this book because I expect most readers of this formatting guide will want to learn about formatting novels.

When I wrote the first edition of this book, most of my book layout experience had been through working for publishers. Since then, I've taken on many more freelance commissions for self-publishing authors. It's been a privilege and an eye-opening one to work with such a diverse group of people. In terms of expertise, these self-publishers range from experienced authors who know how to lay out a book, but know nothing about Createspace, to authors who have taught me something about the commercial side of Createspace but want me to finish off their manuscripts with section breaks, headers and footers and contents page. Then there are the authors who don't even know how to type in a paragraph.

I've written this edition of the book to address the needs of all this diverse group. Doing so creates a problem because topics of vital importance to one reader are of no interest to the next. So I have divided the book into parts. If you are familiar with Createspace and Microsoft Word, I recommend you skim the first three parts – assuring yourself that you already understand these topics – before working through the layout techniques from Part Four.

PART ONE — Selling your book through Createspace: addresses the mechanics of working with Createspace. We look at the commercial side of self-publishing paperbacks, from why you should bother producing a paperback at all through to margins and pricing strategies. Then I answer the most commonly raised questions that my clients ask me, such as whether they should buy their own ISBNs, what is the best trim size, how to link paperback and Kindle editions on Amazon, and how non-US citizens can avoid paying US withholding tax.

PART TWO — A typical book creation workflow: summarizes the rest of this book by running through a typical workflow for producing a paperback, from setting up the project on Createspace.com through when and how to contact cover artists, and down to the detail of setting headers and section breaks. If this is your first self-published paperback book, skim through Part One to grasp the basic concepts of using Createspace, and then use Part Two as your roadmap, dipping into the detail in the rest of the book as you need.

PART THREE — Formatting: setting correct paragraph and page breaks: handles paragraph breaks and page breaks. Most self-publishers already know these techniques, and can skip straight to Part Four, but check first. If setting paragraph breaks is new to you, read Part Three carefully and start acting immediately, because I regret to inform you that you're going to need to make a large number of corrections.

PART FOUR — Formatting: page layout: covers page layout: headers, footers, page numbers, and sections. We explore styles, both how to use them and suggested values to set for paragraph spacing, indentation, justification, font settings, typeface choices and more. This is where the first edition started. If you are familiar with Createspace and basic word processing, then skim the first three parts to verify you already know that material, and then start reading more carefully at Part Four.

PART FIVE — Images: covers all areas of graphics inside books. In addition to photographs and large illustrations, we look at using images as ornaments, including the use of Unicode glyphs.

PART SIX — Details: covers the finishing polish you can apply to book layout, such as scene breaks, drop caps, contents pages, how to curl your quotes, and what to put in your front matter.

PART SEVEN —**Advanced topics** is where I address advanced techniques. For the majority of readers of this book, the topics covered in Part Seven are optional and might not even be relevant, so do not be dismayed if some of this seems complex. Topics include advanced typography (such as kerning and how to avoid faux small caps in Word), colorspaces, dot gain and PDF settings, and the merits of upgrading to newer editions of Microsoft Word, and third party tools, such as Adobe Acrobat Pro and InDesign.

One last thing before we get cracking — I've divided the book into tips and topics, rather than steps or chapters, because there isn't a set sequence to follow (except for Part Two which sets out a workflow). Where I can, I've tried to teach you the fundamentals before moving to the slightly more advanced techniques, but a good way to read this book is as follows:

1. Read from start to finish, preferably with a copy of Word to hand so you can play with the techniques as you go. If you are familiar with Createspace and just want to learn formatting techniques, then skim parts 1 to 3, although there may might be topics you are unfamiliar with.

2. Think about what you need at your stage of readiness for Createspace or wherever you're aiming your book layout.

3. Then go back to the tips that you need the most, and re-read them, exploring the steps with an open copy of Microsoft Word. The best way to learn is through *doing*.

Part 1 – Selling your book through Createspace

How to use Createspace to sell your books •
Common questions about Createspace

WHY BOTHER WITH A PAPERBACK EDITION?

If you're writing mainstream fiction then it's likely that the eBook edition of your book is going to outsell your paperbacks by a significant margin. If you are writing reference books or selling books as a sideline to your main business then your paperback sales will likely be higher.

My own ratios are that the first edition of the book you are reading now has sold even numbers of paperbacks and eBooks, while the novels I publish sell 100 eBooks for every paperback (and most of those eBook sales are through amazon.com).

At this point, if you are a novelist, you might be asking yourself whether producing a paperback edition is a distraction from your core business of writing and selling eBooks. In fact, I would be disappointed if you didn't ask yourself this question because there are many time traps for the unwary self-publisher, and it is a good idea to regularly ask yourself whether you are spending your valuable time where it will give you the greatest return.

Here are a few good reasons to produce a paperback, if you are a novelist:

1. **It allows you to list giveaways through goodreads.com** — this is an important and cheap marketing tool. You can list your book to give away at the increasingly popular site, Goodreads. If you host a few short giveaways over the course of 2-3 months then you could have several thousand people add your book to their Goodreads bookshelves and gain a handful of reviews too. Goodreads currently only allows paperbacks to be listed, not eBooks.

2. **Some reviewers only take paperback books**. Sending your book to reviewers hoping to win quotable reviews is an old and still important marketing tactic. A significant minority of reviewers request only paperbacks are sent. I'm certain that many reviewers set this restriction as a very crude quality bar for you to hurdle. The thinking goes something like this: "The most amateurish books are often eBook only. I might miss a few gems by insisting on paperbacks, but it's worth that risk if it means I waste less of my time reading dross that should never been published." Yes, I've read excellent eBook-only titles myself, but these restrictions tend to come from more established reviewers who

are inundated with review requests and probably desperate to reduce the number of books sent to them.

3. **Some purchasers of eBooks only buy if there is a paperback edition.** This is a common comment on Goodreads and Amazon's community forums. It's the same logic as point 2: for a potential reader considering taking a chance on a new, self-published author, the existence of a paperback is crude evidence of a basic level of professionalism.

4. **Paperbacks could provide a healthy sales channel.** Most self-published fiction authors I've talked with say that paperback sales are limited, but there are a few who say it brings in a significant additional income. Those authors selling well tend to have local independent bookstores or book fairs and/ or they have published a series of books (although with books series, I suspect paperbacks are substitutes for eBooks sales that they would have made anyway)

5. **A paperback edition lends you credibility** — great for interviews with local press (cue picture of you holding your paperback) and your friends, colleagues and chance encounters when you answer the inevitable question: 'have you been published?'

6. **A paperback edition helps your beta reading program.** I worked in the software industry for twenty years and can vouch for the power of peer review, whether of software code, of prose sentences and paragraphs and scenes, or of characters and plot. Getting reaction from readers is vital, and doing so with readers from a different background to you is more likely to raise important issues you need to address that you are blind to. In publishing terms, people who read an early edition of your book are often referred to as beta readers. I run a beta read program for my publishing imprint, Greyhart Press. Volunteers are given a copy of the beta version of the book (paperback or eBook — their choice) and when the final edition is published, volunteers receive the finished paperback edition, which includes a list of beta readers prominently thanked at the start of the book. This is a great system. We get vital feedback, and many of the beta readers enjoy the experience. I don't think they're just being polite either, because many of our beta readers ask to be a part of the next beta read program. After completing the beta program, our team members have often told me how proud they are to have the finished paperback on their bookshelf and with their name prominently displayed at the front. Yes, you could do all of this with just eBooks, but I am convinced that our use of paperbacks here takes motivation and reward to a higher level.

7. **A paperback looks better on your shelf and is future proofed.** It's easy to become overly obsessed with sales figures. It's important to feel the

satisfaction too in having crafted something you're proud of. I've published around thirty paperbacks myself and other publishers have published my fiction in hardback. When I glance at my office bookshelf and see all those books I am so proud to have produced, I get a glow in my heart. I've produced many more than thirty eBooks but they don't give me the same satisfaction as the rows of my paperbacks on my bookshelf. In sixty years' time, I don't expect I'll be in a position to glance at anything, but I like to think my immediate family will have some of my paperbacks on their shelves. They will have digital versions of my books too, but consider this: I was an early adopter of eBooks, paying good money for Microsoft Reader format eBooks and reading them on Windows Mobile devices. Only a decade later and both the book format and the device category are now dead, my eBooks impossible to read unless I drag out my old laptop. On the other hand, I have printed books that are over a century old...

How to use Createspace to print and sell your book

I'm going to quickly run through some of the ways you can use Createspace to sell your book. If you already know how you're going to do this, skip straight to Part 2, where we'll start to cover how you prepare your book for Createspace.

I've listed several selling methods separately, but they are not mutually exclusive: you can combine them.

1. Let Amazon sell them for you

For most authors, especially fiction authors, this is the most likely way you can make money and the easiest too. Here's how it works.

1. Set up a book project on Createspace, define your book's content, and once you're happy with your proof copy, tell Createspace you're ready to publish.
2. Your book will be available for customers to buy from Createspace.com. Not many people go shopping for books there, so what happens usually within 24 hours is far more interesting — your book will appear on Amazon for people out in the real world to buy.
3. For English-language books, the most important places your books will appear will be in the Books section of amazon.com and amazon.co.uk The book will also appear at other European sites, such as Amazon.de, but at the time of writing will not appear immediately on the Canadian amazon.ca, although it might do later. [see the section on Canadian distribution on page 39].

Suppose someone in Boston, Massachusetts, goes to amazon.com, likes the look of your book, and presses the BUY button. Here's what happens:

- Amazon processes the transaction, taking the money and sending the order to Createspace to print the book. Createspace will have the book printed and distributed. Usually they will do both themselves from their HQ in South Carolina.

- Createspace will handle the packaging and posting, wrapping the book in Amazon.com branded packaging and sending it off to the customer in Boston.
- The book arrives in Boston and the customer reads your masterpiece. Createspace under promise distribution times to keep on the safe side. Usually the customer will receive the book about 4-6 days after hitting that BUY button.
- By now, your Createspace account dashboard will be showing the sale to Boston and have updated the running total of that month's royalties, and royalties due. If you've made a minimum sales amount ($20) then you will be paid either at the end of the current month or the next, depending on when the sales were reported. (Sales take months to be reported and paid through any channels *other* than amazon.com, amazon.co.uk, Createspace.com and the European amazon stores).

I explain more about royalties and margins on [page 36] but here's a summary now: Start with the price the customer paid. Take off any sales tax. Take off the cost to print and distribute the book. Of what's left, 40% goes to Amazon and 60% goes to you. That's a better royalty rate than you will get through any other book retailer, and a vastly better rate than is earned by mainstream authors such as Stephen King and Dan Brown (but, of course, they will sell far more copies than you unless you hit it really lucky).

Although you will see the sale to Boston straight away, all you will know is that a sale has come through amazon.com. You never know the name or address of the customer.

It's probably a good idea to do some promotional work on your book. However, some self-published authors argue that *the best thing you can do for the first few books is to move straight on to writing the next book.* If that's what you want to do, Createspace makes it easy.

The Amazon KDP service through which you can publish your Kindle edition works essentially the same way. You can completely ignore your first book while you write your second, only glancing at your bank statement on occasion to see the money paid in from your book royalties. Of course, you still need to declare your earnings when working out your tax return, but even there, Createspace (and Amazon KDP) make it simple to work out your earnings.

I made the point that our customer was in Boston Massachusetts. If you yourself are American, everything has stayed in America, and all the money has been in

US dollars. But Createspace and Amazon KDP (for Kindles, remember?) are international although not nearly as international as your potential English language readership.

Canada is annoying when it comes to Createspace and book distribution in general because it always seems to me to be more difficult than it should be, although getting easier. [More on Canada on page 39].

But with the UK, the international nature of Createspace works well.

Suppose you are an American author, but this time the customer doesn't live in Boston, Massachusetts, they are in Boston, Lincolnshire and press the Buy button on amazon.co.uk. In this case, the book will be printed and shipped by Createspace in the UK from the new city of Milton Keynes (I know it well — I once lived there!). The cost to print and ship is slightly more than with Createspace's US operation, but the difference isn't enormous and the result is the same, except on your Createspace royalty report, instead of adding to the running total of US dollars, the purchase adds to your total of GB pounds. And if the customer lives in Barcelona, you will see an increase in your Euro balance.

You can set various options in your Createspace account about how various currencies are paid. I live in the UK and Createspace pays into my bank account in dollars, Euros, and pounds, with my bank levying a small charge for each currency conversion.

One other aspect of selling your book through Amazon is worth mentioning here. If you change your book (for example, to correct a spelling mistake or to add a reference to your sequel that you've just published) then it is very quick and easy to update your book project so long as you distribute your book only through Amazon and have not selected the extended distribution option. If you have wider distribution, you may have to pay a charge for each update and your changed version can take weeks to work its way through the system until customers can buy it.

Summary: selling your book through Amazon

In most respects this is far easier and pays far better than the traditional model for small publishers selling books through national bookstores.

But that is the drawback for some authors. This route won't get you into bookstores, although you might if you select extended distribution. See option 3a below...

Letting Amazon sell your book is an approach that you can combine nicely with selling yourself directly.

2. Sell them yourself

Createspace allows you to buy books directly from them at cost price. The shipping costs are fairly cheap (although the packaging isn't always as secure as with other suppliers) and you don't need to buy many copies to make shipping costs viable to sell at a profit.

For example, let's take a typical scenario. To buy 10 copies of a 250 page paperback directly from Createspace and ship to a continental US address currently costs $4.65 per book ($3.85 printing + $0.80 shipping). To buy 5,000 copies of the same book costs $4.25 ($3.85 + $0.40 shipping). But why bother overwhelming your house with boxes of books, because to buy 50 costs $4.31 ($3.85 +$0.46 shipping)?

Try out pricing scenarios for yourself with the online Createspace price calculator. From the main Createspace homepage, click on 'Books' from the top menu and then 'Publish a Trade Paperback'. The printing & shipping costs for buying copies directly is under the 'Buying Copies' tab.

Here's the bad news if you live outside of the US: the books that *you* order from Createspace are always printed in America. So long as you can accept ship times of about 6 weeks, the cost to ship over the Atlantic to Europe and the UK is modest enough to leave you a large profit margin. Even for Canadians, the profit margin is still large, even though it costs more to ship books from America to Canada than it does to ship them to the UK (and costs even more if your shipment is held up at customs).

Once your books have been delivered, you can sell them however you like. For example:

- Sell them as a complement to your normal business. This works well for non-fiction that ties into your consultancy and counselling work. For example, I formatted a range of books for an Australian relationship counsellor who buys her own books directly from Createspace in the US and sells them to her clients in Australia.

- Sell them directly from your website. This tends to work best if your book is non-fiction. Suppose you have a 100,000 hits-per-day website about market tips for trading in stocks & bonds. You might write a book explaining your trading strategies. The easiest thing to do would be to put a link on your webpage that connects through to the Amazon/ Createspace and other sales pages. But you could also add a shopping cart facility to your website and handle the book shipment yourself. It would be more work, but higher margin for you.

- Sell from independent and local bookstores, local stores of any type, libraries, and tourist attraction gift stores. It's worth trying this, especially if you have a strong local angle, perhaps a historical romance set in your home town. Don't be surprised to find your independent store isn't as independent as you think and might not take your book unless they can order through a national distribution network.

- Contact local writers' groups and join in with anything they do that involves selling its members' books. If your local group doesn't do any selling, why not organize them to start now?

- Sell books at literary events. I've launched or been launched at several science fiction and fantasy conventions in the UK, such as Eastercon (science fiction) and Fantasycon (actually, horror mostly, despite the name). There are many such conventions all over the world, although you must be realistic that if you are an unknown author, you will be competing for attention against big name authors in the convention's genre.

- Friends, family, and co-workers. Do encourage your friends to write a good review on Amazon etc. if they like your book. Consider giving away some books, because when you're starting out, good reviews on amazon.com are probably worth more to you than book sales. Some people are far more likely to read and review a paperback than an eBook emailed to them.

- Booksigning tours of bookstores. For this you need to set yourself up as a small publisher as many chains won't allow you to bring a box of books to sell; they have to order through their central ordering system.

That's a lot of ways to sell your book. I hope you're feeling enthusiastic at this point, eager to get out and sell those books. So I feel a little shamefaced because I'm going to puncture that enthusiasm a tad.

People publish books for lots of reasons. I'm going to assume a big part of why you are publishing your book is because you want to make some money, because if that isn't a good description of your goals, then what I'm about to say doesn't apply to you.

I've known many authors who sell their books directly.

Of those who make a useful income doing so, almost all are selling non-fiction that ties into their successful business selling some kind of consultancy or advice, such as my stock picker and relationship counsellor examples.

For fiction authors to make a profit, you need to be a natural seller, have a book that is in a popular mainstream genre (such as thrillers), be prepared to put in a lot of time, and be lucky enough to have local venues through which you can sell a useful number of books.

When you cost in their time, most fiction authors lose money on direct sales of their books. The best way for them to approach direct sales is an adventure. Take out the cost of your time and chalk up that time instead to your entertainment. Instead of watching the game this weekend, go sell your book instead. With that attitude, Createspace works very well indeed, because you don't need to buy batches of thousands of book, as you used to before the days of high quality print-on-demand books.

At least if you put your bookselling down to entertainment you can enjoy yourself safe in the knowledge that if you sell enough copies to cover their costs then you aren't losing money. That's a better approach to setting yourself up as a traditional small publisher, as we'll see in the next section, because that's a route to losing real money, no matter how you account for it.

3. Set yourself up as a traditional small publisher

If your primary aim is to sell books that you have written yourself, then you will have a hard time persuading the publishing industry you are a genuine small publisher. However, some writers do manage this and moving up from self- to small publisher can open access to more reviewers and retailers. Most writers will find this approach is far more trouble that it is worth. Why go down this route when Createspace does so much of this for you?

I don't advise this route, but I'll describe it anyway for comparison.

Back in the days before print-on-demand services such as Createspace started to produce decent quality books, you could set yourself up as a small publisher. Some people still do and are very successful with this model. However, if you are self-publishing, you should be aware from the start that most retailers and wholesalers will want to deal with publishers who publish more than one author and who have a range of several books. Some authors self-publish and place their books in book stores anyway by being — how shall we say? — flexible with the truth.

Here's what you would do:

- o Buy/ acquire ISBN numbers from your national ISBN agency and register yourself as a publisher.
- o Apply to be registered with a national wholesaler. These are the organizations who take orders from bookstores and pass on the books that you have given the wholesaler. In the US, major wholesalers are Ingram and Baker & Taylor; in the UK the equivalents are Bertrams and Gardners. It is possible to persuade the head office of major retailers to let you sell books to them directly rather than go through a wholesaler, but you will need to have a seriously good reason why they should make an exception for you. Rather than deal with tens of thousands of small and self-publishers, large retailers much prefer to order through a handful of wholesalers (and distributors — who are another type of organization, but won't deal with you unless you are already selling books by the ton, or have some other seriously compelling selling point).

Then

EITHER

Approach a printer to put in a book order.

Order a batch of books from your printer, typically at least a 100 copies for digital printing (which is what Createspace uses), and more likely 5,000 for traditional offset litho printing (which is how the big publishers print books – cost per book is less and the binding can be slightly better quality, but the minimum print run is larger).

OR

Set up an account with a print-on demand service who allows retailers to return unsold books, a key requirement for retailers. Lightning Source International allows this; Createspace does not. Many wholesalers and retailers say they do not accept books from print-on-demand services.

DO expect resistance on the grounds that you aren't a 'proper' publisher.

DON'T expect retailers to stock your book, just because you have gone through the hoops that allow bookstore managers to order your book.

If you've succeeded in getting through those steps and are working with a wholesaler such as Bertrams or Ingram, then your wholesaler will provide you with an online ordering tool which will notify you when they want you to post them a batch of books. Lightning Source International will organize this for you on your behalf.

3a. Using Createspace's 'Expanded Distribution' option

You can opt (for free) to put your title into Createspace's Expanded Distribution sales channel, which means they will list your book with US book wholesalers. In other words, it exposes your book to the US national book ordering system and that means US bookstores can see it and find it and order it. If I go into a Barnes & Noble in, say, New York then I can tell a member of staff that I want your Expanded Distribution book but I can't see it on the shelves. The bookseller will then log onto their ordering system and place an order for me. Result!

However there's a *big* difference between making your book available to order and having it listed so that the store manager is allowed to stock it. Barnes & Noble in particular seems reluctant at present to stock Createspace titles. And even if they were allowed to stock the book, why would they? Barnes & Noble in the US, and Waterstones in the UK for that matter, seem to stumble along as zombie businesses only one crisis away from going under. If I were running a business in deep trouble, I don't think I could afford the time to talk to self-publishing authors let alone stock their books. Not unless there was an immediately compelling reason why I think your book would sell.

Now comes the key cost of the Expanded Distribution channel: the cost to the customer. With the Expanded Distribution channel, you get a margin after Createspace's costs of 40%. For sales through amazon, you get a margin of 60%. That might not sound much, but in practice it means that for an average-sized novel, if you select the Expanded Distribution channel then your book will need to be somewhat expensive compared to undiscounted books from major publishers. Without Expanded Distribution, your book can undercut the undiscounted books from major publishers.

Let's look at some numbers:

I self-publish a mini-series of novels through Createspace. The first one is 318 pages at a 6" x 9" trim size. It's about 125,000 words. List price is $11, which is aggressively priced against similar books from major publishers that would typically have a list price of $15. However, in bookstores (both online and brick-and-mortar) many books are discounted to perhaps $11 or $12, and then there are the mass market paperback that are made as cheaply as possible and with small type but might be priced at $7 or $8. I can never compete with $7 books by using Createspace, but at $11 I'm competitive against premium books. For sales through amazon.com, I make a profit of $1.94 per book. I can't sell that book through Expanded Distribution because my list price isn't enough to cover costs.

Suppose I upped my list price to $11.69. That's the minimum list price that allows me to sell through Expanded Distribution. At that slightly higher price I would make $2.35 on each sale through amazon.com and through Expanded Distribution I would make a profit of $0.01. That's not a typo, that's once cent profit per book.

Of course, you might not feel you need to be aggressive in your pricing. Perhaps you expect to make significant sales at author events and would prefer a higher list price printed on the back of your book because then you could buy directly from Createspace and offer big discounts to people buying your book at your events. The printing cost to buy direct is $4.66 (plus shipping).

Here are the stats for my 318 page book. Prices calculated September 2013.

List Price ($)	Amazon.com sales channel royalty ($)	Expanded Distribution channel royalty ($)	US market notes
11.00	1.94	N/A	Equivalent to discounted mainstream paperback novel.
11.69	2.35	0.01	
15.00	4.34	1.34	Undiscounted mainstream paperback novel.
20.00	7.34	3.34	Very expensive for a self-published novel. Viable for some non-fiction.

Expanded Distribution summary:

Opting for Expanded Distribution can get you listed for book stores to order and possibly even stock your book. Your margin for books sold through this channel will be lower, and that may mean *you need to raise the list price for books sold through all channels.* That might be a big problem, or might not matter... depends on your pricing strategy.

4. And still more ways to sell your book ...

I have deliberately simplified many aspects of selling books. For example, you can, of course, print and distribute your book exclusively through Lightning Source and have them sell your books through amazon.com. Lightning Source also allow you to set your own discount, but they will also charge you more fees and are really set up for working with publishers rather than self-publishing authors who have little knowledge of the publishing industry.

There are lively discussions online about various publishing models. Join an author collective (such as the Indie Writers Unite group on Facebook) or a Goodreads author group and ask for advice.

Conclusion: How YOU should sell YOUR book!

If you're based in the US then Createspace is the best print-on-demand service for you. Createspace is the simplest, fastest, and cheapest way to get your book into the amazon online store AND the fastest way to deliver books to your customers.

Going with Createspace now does not prevent you from moving to another printer or distribution model at a later date. Dealing with wholesalers and the head offices of major book stores as you are starting out is going to weigh you down in complexity and cost for little or no benefit, especially if you write fiction. You're much better off writing your next book.

If you're US based then you can turn the page now to the next section. For self-publishers elsewhere in the world, life is slightly more complicated, so you need to stick around for another few paragraphs.

If you are based outside the US and think you can sell significant copies of your book yourself and at a premium price (which means you are probably selling non-fiction) then you could let Createspace handle the online orders and approach a local printer to supply copies directly. They might be more expensive than Createspace, but won't have to ship across the Atlantic. For example, in the UK, you could try Berforts Information Press Ltd. I've not used them myself, but one of the imprints who publish my fiction does and the quality is very high.

If you're based in Canada, the advantage is more nuanced but still there. If you select Createspace Expanded Distribution, you will probably have your paperback listed on amazon.ca (though there is no guarantee) but you are unlikely to have your book in the Indigo chain. You *can* get a listing on Indigo through a company called iUniverse. And by listing I mean that Indigo store managers are allowed to stock your book, and not that they *will* stock your book. iUniverse is an outfit who will charge you a minimum $899 upfront fee for what Createspace offers for free or you can do yourself for a fraction of the price, and pays out lower royalty rates than Createspace. At the end of the process, there is no reason why using iUniverse would gain you a single additional sale.

If you're based in Australia, then Createspace does not service your home market. I advise you to use Createspace to supply North America and Europe, and consider a local supplier for the Australian market (LSI does have an Australian presence). In November 2013, Amazon launched an Australian Kindle Store, so I'll keep an eye on this as I think it's possible that Createspace will follow their parent into Australia.

COMMON QUESTIONS ABOUT CREATESPACE

I've worked with many authors to produce paperbacks and eBooks. I am often asked the same questions. In this section I've written out those questions together with my answers.

What is an ISBN and do I need one?

You will see may references to ISBNs in this section, so let's start at the beginning and explain what they are.

ISBN stands for International Standard Book Number and is a way of labeling every edition of every book with a unique number. Given that a popular book, such as *To Kill a Mockingbird*, may have been published in several hundred editions and by multiple publishers in multiple countries and in many languages, you will appreciate that the publishing industry worked out many years ago that using just the title and author to identify a book is not good enough.

If you walk into a brick and mortar bookstore and order a book, the assistant will use an ISBN to place your order. The order might be sent to a wholesaler who checks stock levels for that ISBN and places an order with a distributor. The distributor in turn might note that sales projections predict that they will soon run out of stock, and so contact the publisher to warn that stock levels are depleting and perhaps they should consider another print run for that book. All the way through the system everyone — bookstore, wholesaler, distributor, publisher, printer — everyone uses the ISBN to identify which edition of which book they are talking about.

It isn't only the business of buying and selling that uses ISBNs. Librarything, Goodreads, library services, US Copyright Office, British Library, some reviewers and advertising services and many other organizations require an ISBN too.

So, yes, ISBNs are very important and your paperback will definitely need one. You have no choice if you use Createspace because they force you to have one,

eason. If you printed a book without an ISBN, most of the book
...l refuse to touch your book.

...rmat, the ISBN is a 10- or 13-digit number. These are sometimes
refer... s ISBN-10 and ISBN-13. The 10 digit is the old standard ISBN format
and the 13-digit is the newer format that has mostly replaced ISBN-10s. Some
books have both. If you have an option to deal with 10- or 13- digit ISBNs,
always work with the ISBN-13.

In the traditional way of publishing (by which I mean before print-on-demand
services such as Createspace) you would start off by registering your
PUBLISHING IMPRINT with your NATIONAL ISBN AGENCY, and acquiring a block
of ISBN numbers, usually 100 ISBNs.

To register your imprint, you need to supply your imprint's name and contact
details so that someone enquiring about your book (for example, to order
copies) have a route to you, the publisher. The block of ISBN numbers assigned
to you are linked forever to your publishing imprint.

I myself have a publishing imprint called Greyhart Press. When I registered, I
was given 100 ISBN numbers. Someone in the publishing industry can type in
any of my ISBNs into an ISBN database tool and immediately know that ISBN
is associated with Greyhart Press, and then look up my contact details.

For this reason, sharing ISBNs between different people is a bad idea. At best
you are likely to cause confusion, and at worst Createspace and your ISBN
agency will refuse to deal with you.

*Figure 1: A Createspace-printed paperback showing the
ISBN as a barcode at bottom-right. This ISBN is forever
associated with the Greyhart Press imprint.*

The publisher identified inside the ISBN is
called the PUBLISHER OF RECORD. This is
important with Createspace, because the
simplest option is to let Createspace give
you a free ISBN. Those free ISBNs are paid
for by Createspace who buy in bulk and so
can buy them for much cheaper than you
can. Now, as we've just seen, blocks of
ISBNs are linked to a publishing imprint at
the point they are issued by the national
ISBN agency. Naturally, Createspace can't

know who will use their free ISBNs, and yet they must give a publisher imprɪ when they buy the ISBNs. So they use their own. It's called *Createspace Independent Publishing Platform*.

When I first published paperback books for Greyhart Press, I used the free Createspace ISBNs. The cover spine, back cover, and title page all have the Greyhart Press logo. The copyright page inside the book says 'Published by Greyhart Press'. I make no reference at all to Createspace. However, if you looked up our older books at online stores such as amazon.com, WHSmith.co.uk or Barnes & Noble, they will all list the publisher as 'Createspace Independent Publishing Platform'.

Does this matter? Well, that's for you to decide. Some self-publishing authors feel that making up a publishing imprint and using their own ISBNs gives them more credibility. Some attempt to hide the fact that their books are self-published and others are open about it, despite registering their own ISBN. On the other hand, many authors are perfectly happy to take the free ISBN from Createspace.

For my own case, I doubt whether registering Greyhart Press and using my own ISBNs makes any difference to the sales of the books I publish. I only registered because I was at one point a founder member of a collective of small press publishers that stipulated as a requirement that their members had registered their publishing imprints with our national ISBN agency.

ɔok world, most retailers other than Amazon require ISBNs for
.oo. (And the eBook editions need different ISBNs from your
paperʋack). A popular way to handle distribution to all the major eBook
retailers other than Amazon is through a company called Smashwords.
They offer a free ISBN just as Createspace does for paperbacks. If you
use their ISBN then the publisher of record will be listed as *Smashwords
Inc.*

For my Greyhart Press imprint, I always take the free ISBN from
Smashwords.

In some countries (certainly this is true of the USA) Createspace offers a middle
ground. They call this CUSTOM ISBN. You pay some money (currently $10) and
buy an ISBN from Createspace that allows you to alter the publisher of record.
In other words, when you look at your book's sales page on amazon.com, it lists
the publisher as whatever you tell Createspace instead of 'Createspace
Independent Publishing Platform' (which is how the publisher would be listed
if you took the free ISBN).

Custom ISBNs are not available in the UK where my imprint is based, so I've
no personal experience of using them.

Thinking of registering a publishing imprint? Each country has its own national
ISBN agency authorized by the international ISBN organization. If you Google
for 'ISBN agency', you will soon find yours. Usually you have to pay to acquire
ISBNs and register your imprint, but in a few countries (Canada is one), you can
acquire ISBNs for free (or rather your fellow taxpayers are subsidizing you, so
I wouldn't brag about it ☺)

Should I use my own ISBNs or use one from Createspace?

I see this question all the time, which is why I separated it out from and slightly
duplicated the 'what is an ISBN' subject, so you can zoom straight here. The
popularity of this question is also why you should Google around because
people are debating this all the time.

My advice is that registering your imprint is of practical benefit in these
circumstances:

- You intend to use more than one printer for the same book or otherwise have more complex distribution arrangements.
- You are a small publisher, rather than a self-publisher (in other words, your primary operation is publishing authors other than yourself). This is simply because your authors (including potential authors looking you up before submitting) may feel you are more of a 'proper' publisher.
- If you feel that having a registered imprint gives you credibility and are attempting to obscure the fact that you are self-publishing your books. If you are based in the US, then you can achieve the same effect by using Createspace's 'Custom ISBN' option for ISBNs. This costs you $10 and lets you associate your own imprint name with your book. It's something that is only available in the US.

Otherwise, I personally wouldn't bother. ISBNs are a critical tool that allows the publishing industry of printers, distributors, wholesalers, retailers and others to communicate with one another. But one of the quiet advantages of publishing through Createspace is that this entire world is taken care for you.

When you upload your book to your Createspace account from the laptop in your apartment in Chicago and someone in London, England buys your paperback a week later, who prints the book? Who puts it in the post? Who collects the money from the transaction? Who pays any sales taxes? Well, I know the answer to the last two questions is Amazon Europe based in Luxemburg, but I don't know nor care about the answers to the other questions. The point is, it works and you don't need to know how it works.

Registering your imprint is something you can come back and do later, if you want to. If you're just starting out then for most authors it's a distraction. You're better off concentrating on writing the next book.

Can I use the same ISBN for my eBook and my paperback?

According to the ISBN rules, no you can't. Each format your book comes in, should have its own ISBN. So if you have a hardback, 6in. x 9in. paperback, and a 5 1/4 in. x 8 1/4 in. paperback, then you need three ISBNs. If you also have an ePUB version then that requires an ISBN too. In theory a Kindle version would also require its own ISBN, but while Kindle books sold through Amazon can be given an ISBN if you really want to, it serves no purpose.

So they are the rules. But should you care? Ethics aside, if you break the rules you are going to risk annoying a lot of people — such as retailers, distributors, and Goodreads librarians — whom you need on your side and you need far more than they need you.

If I print my book with Createspace, do I still own my book?

Yes, you do. I've read alarmist reports online from people trying to scare you into believing that printing a book through Createspace means signing away rights. Don't listen to these people; they are writing absolute nonsense because they think it will attract web traffic.

The only sense in which you do not own everything in your Createspace project is if you accept a free ISBN number from Createspace. You aren't supposed to use that ISBN to print with another printer. What Createspace wants you to do is neither here nor there. It is the national ISBN organizations who state that you shouldn't be using that ISBN anywhere else. I've explained why elsewhere in this section; the point I want to make here is that far from Createspace stealing your rights, Createspace themselves are not permitted let you use their ISBNs with other printers.

If I print my book with Createspace, can I also print it with another printer?

Absolutely. The only restriction is that if you have taken a free ISBN offered by Createspace, then you need to use a new ISBN for your other printer. If you have the ISBN listed on the copyright page of your paperback (which I advise you to do as some distributors insist on this) then you will need to change your interior to list the new ISBN. If you expect to use several printers then it may be a better idea to buy your own ISBNs, which you can use with as many printers as you like.

Some people do work with multiple printers, using Createspace as the international and online storefront for their books, but using a local printer for books to supply books that they then sell directly.

I do need to caution you, though, because if you use the same ISBN number with different distributors then you could wind up with a confusing mess. Suppose you took your ISBN and printed the same book with the same ISBN through Createspace, Lulu, and Lightning Source International. Once your book had made it into the ordering systems of the publishing industry, what would happen when a potential reader walks into a bookstore and asks the bookseller to order your book? Which version would be ordered?

I'm not sure what would happen. I know I have seen Lulu and Createspace editions of the same book on an amazon.com sales page, listed as two separate editions. I'm not saying this would necessarily cause a problem, but if you go solely through Createspace, they are not merely printing the book but (assuming you select at least one channel in your book project) acting as your distributor too. And by distributing straight to Amazon you get fast access straight to the most important online retailer in the world. How your book gets from your Createspace book project to the Amazon sales page, and how Amazon handles the sales, takes the money, and passes it back to Createspace... all that happens automatically. You can treat it as a black box: book in; sales report and royalties out.

On the other hand, if you sell through book distributors other than Createspace, then you will need to look in more detail at the mechanics of how that works and what your responsibilities are as a publisher listed with your local ISBN agency.

If I make changes to my book, do I need to use a new ISBN/ new edition number?

If you make substantive changes, yes. But the meaning of *substantive* is vague. If you change trim size, or completely new cover art, then yes you certainly need a new ISBN. If you've spotted a handful of typos and want to quietly correct them, then no you don't need a new ISBN or refer to a new edition. Indeed, I would keep as quiet as you can about fixing mistakes.

The book you are reading now is the second edition. Right now, I'm estimating the wordcount for the finished book will be around triple the first edition, and that means I'm going to use a new ISBN for the second edition and mark it clearly as a second edition.

Do I have to upload my book to Createspace as a PDF or can I upload a Word .doc or other format?

I advise uploading as a PDF. If you don't produce a PDF file yourself, then Createspace will create one for you and that's such a vital process that I would want that under my control. However, Createspace (and Lulu, but not Lightning Source) do allow you to upload Word files instead of PDFs (and then automatically create PDFs). This hasn't worked well in my limited experience, with headers and footers losing alignment and page breaks occurring at different points in the text. Since I was already set up for producing PDFs, I rapidly abandoned attempts to use Word docs instead. [I explore this in more detail on p191].

Copyright, Library of Congress, and mandatory deposit

Summary:

You automatically have copyright in your book, but consider registering your book with the US Electronic Copyright Office so that you can prove this.

If your book is on sale in the US, you are required by US law to send 2 copies of your paperback to the US Copyright Office.

If your book is on sale in the UK, you are required by UK law to send 1 copy of your paperback to the British Library Deposit Service.

If you write a book, you are the copyright holder for that work. You don't have to register somewhere; you don't have to do anything: it's automatic. The problem, of course, is if some unscrupulous little %$##!! copies your book and publishes it under his or her own name. Being entitled to your copyright is rarely an issue: it's whether you can prove you hold the copyright that matters.

Copyright theft is still very rare, but the ease with which people can turn a stolen manuscript into a published Kindle book on Amazon within less than 24 hours means it's easier to do these days, and I suspect blatant copyright theft is on the increase.

Createspace, Amazon and the other retailers say they're on your side, but the reality is that they don't have the resources or motivation to get themselves embroiled in tricky legal disputes. If you're worried about copyright theft, you can do things to prove you own the work and this might (and I did say might) persuade Createspace and the rest that you are the clear owner of the work.

Is it the Library of Congress or the Copyright Office that I should be dealing with?

The United States Copyright Office is a department of the Library of Congress. Small and self-publishers will normally only need to deal with the Copyright Office. Find it on the web here: **www.copyright.gov**

Here are some things you can do or should do:

Register copyright with the US Copyright Office (optional). You can now register your book with the electronic copyright office (eCO) (here: http://www.copyright.gov/register/literary.html). Fill in the online form, pay the fee (currently $35) and send a copy of the book. If you haven't yet published the book in print, you can simply upload a PDF of your book at the same time as you register it. Easy! If the book is already published in paperback you need to send physical copies and include a tracking sheet with your book. My advice is to register the book shortly before you publish. This could be essential evidence if you need to prove that your book belongs to you.

Deposit your book with the US Copyright Office (mandatory). US law requires you to send two copies of your paperback as their mandatory deposit program. See http://www.copyright.gov/mandatory/index.html

Deposit your book with the British Library depository service (mandatory). If you publish a book in the UK, you are required by law to send a copy of your book to the British Library deposit service (see http://www.bl.uk/aboutus/legaldeposit/) within a month of publication. In Createspace terms, if you tick the channel box to say you want to distribute to Amazon Europe, that means *you* are responsible for sending a copy of your book to the British Library.

If you don't do this, does that mean a British bobby will knock on your door and ask you to accompany them to their police station? Well, I don't think that's likely! I've not heard of sanctions for overseas publishers, but if you are a UK publisher and have registered your imprint with Nielsen, the UK ISBN agency, then they *will* check up on whether you are sending your books to the deposit library.

Even if you're based outside of the UK, if you are worried about unscrupulous people stealing your work and passing it off as theirs, then it can only help to have a little proof on your side. There are unscrupulous Brits too, you know. Oh, yes!

What about Library of Congress CIP numbers? If you pick up a book published in the USA by a large publisher, you will see a Library of Congress reference number (a 'CIP' number) on the copyright page, and you'll naturally wonder how to get one. The thing is, unless you're a large publisher, the Library of Congress doesn't want to know about you. That's right. Not only are you not required to send a copy of your book to register it with the Library of Congress, they ask that you don't try.

What about Canada?

Disclaimer: *I'm not a lawyer and you should consider the following to be an opinion and not as qualified advice*. The Canadian legal deposit laws only apply to books *published* in Canada, whereas the US and UK laws apply to books *on sale* in those countries, no matter where the publisher (or author) is domiciled or where the books are printed.

My understanding is that in practical terms you must make a legal deposit of your books to the Canadian authorities only if you are domiciled in Canada and have registered your own imprint (i.e. have your own ISBN number) using an ISBN issued by the Canadian authorities. If you are domiciled elsewhere but sell your book into Canada, there is no legal deposit requirement.

Do I <u>really</u> have to send mandatory deposit paperbacks?

The law certainly says you do, but what happens to publishers who don't? In the US you can be fined up to $2,500 for refusal to deposit books.

I know of small and self-publishers who wait to be asked for deposit copies, and in some cases the request never comes. I've not encountered anyone telling me they have been fined. In fact the current US Copyright Office guidance (circular 7D) states that it hopes publishers will send books voluntarily, but if they are forced to send a letter telling you to make a deposit, you still have 3 months to comply before they fine you. On the other hand, once they send you a demand, you have more paperwork and bureaucracy to negotiate.

Yet fulfilling mandatory deposit requirements voluntarily is not something that requires any paperwork. All you have to do is send the books.

My advice is order a couple of copies for the US Copyright office and one for the British Library. Order copies directly from Createspace to send them to the respective deposit libraries. Takes a few minutes. Job done!

How much royalty/margin will I make?

We've seen price examples in action in the previous section, but they are worth repeating:

Take an example book of 250 pages 6" x 9" trim size. This would be typical for a short-ish novel. The 6x9 trim isn't typical for traditional publishing, but see trim size section on [p51] for why you might do this.

Currently, if I look on amazon.com, the typical mainstream paperback retails for $15. If you price your book at $15 then your royalty is $5.15 at amazon.com and $2.15 through expanded distribution. Your UK sales through amazon.co.uk will come in at about £2.54 (about $3.90 before any currency conversion charges from your bank).

But many books on amazon.com are discounted, typically to $10. At that price, Createspace currently pays $2.15 for books sold through amazon.com and $0.15 through expanded distribution.

Some traditionally published books are heavily discounted as mass market paperbacks. These deliberately use cheap paper stock and squeeze the text size, leading, and margins to minimize the page count. Taking an average at amazon.com I would put this price point at around $7. At this price, your book would make 35 cents at amazon.com. You could not sell it through expanded distribution through other book stores (your royalty would be minus $1.05), nor could you sell it at amazon.co.uk (again, you would have a negative royalty, which Createspace will not permit).

Should I choose cream or white paper?

This is a matter of taste. White means bleached white, the same kind of paper that comes out of a photocopier or that you put into your inkjet printer at home. With major publishers, white paper such as this is common for technical books. It looks crisp and modern, which is why I chose white for the paperback edition of the book you are reading now.

Some people hate white paper. I have to say that I've only heard this extreme distaste of white paper stock come from authors, and on the basis that it looks too similar to something they could have printed themselves out of their inkjet or laser printer at home.

Which brings is to 'cream' paper, which stains the paper in an attempt to make it look similar to the paper stock you would see in traditionally printed books. Be clear, though, that the paper stock used by Createspace for their digital printing is not the same as the kind of paper that is used in traditional printing (large print runs for traditional printers use what is called offset litho printing). However, it does look closer to a traditionally printed book. Although it's called 'cream', don't imagine it looks the same color as the kind of thick liquid you might pour over a bowl of strawberries. It's more of a nicotine-stain color

Of course, as I'll be recommending throughout this book, the best way to decide is to see for yourself. Create dummy book projects made up with your potential font/ layout choices, and do one in each paper color too.

Which trim size should I choose?

'Trim Size' means the size of each page as it appears in the final book. It's such an important term, it is worth getting used to. The paperback edition of the book you are reading has a trim size of 6 inches x 9 inches (meaning the pages are 6 inches across and 9 high). That's a very popular size for fiction as well as non-fiction and is a common industry size used by major publishers for premium paperbacks.

Another common size is 5.25in x 8in. This is closer to the conventional mass paperback trim size.

You can go higher: 8in x 10in is possible with Createspace but it is very large and will stand out in a reader's collection as different from other paperbacks. It's more of a coffee table book, which might be just what you want for your travelogue book to do justice to all your color photos you want to show off.

I've also used 5in x 8in for novelettes and novellas (small books of 15-30 thousand words). This looks distinctive and looks good with books that have too low a page count to allow for spine text.

So which size should you pick? As always, I can guide you but there is no substitute for creating mockup book projects for sizes you are considering and get them printed. The way the book feels as you open the pages does depend partly on page count. So in this case, do a very rough layout of your book to get the pagecount right when making up your trial book projects (smaller trim size will mean more pages).

For full-sized novels (about 90k+ words), my preference is for 6in x 9in. For short novels 5.25in x 8in in. For novelettes and shorter novellas, 5in x 8in.

I prefer the 6in x 9in. size for these reasons:

- 6x9 is used by major publishers as the standard size for premium paperbacks. I think you should use every opportunity to show that you should be taken seriously as an author of professional-quality books, and using the 6x9 trim size is a simple way to associate your book in the reader's mind with a high quality product.

- Createspace charge printing costs per page. If you have a larger trim size, you will (probably) fit more words on the page and so have a smaller page count. This increases your profit margin per book. Make sure to read the next topic in this section about changing trim size...
- I find the way the pages open on a 6x9 book from Createspace feels better than with the same book at 5.25 x 8. Why not try it for yourself?

If I change my trim size, should I lay out my book differently?

See previous point about choosing trim size, if you don't know what that term means.

You won't normally need to change trim size, but some people don't like their first choice and change their minds. This is a common scenario with major publishers who will make a hardback, premium trade paperback and mass market paperback for the same book.

If you keep the same font size, margins and line spacing, then you will fit more words into a page of 6x9 trim size than a page of 5.25 x 8. In fact you will fit in more than you probably think as the margin size remains the same and takes up much less proportionally of the larger page.

More words per page means fewer pages; fewer pages means lower print costs; lower print cost means either higher margin for you or a lower retail price. So that's good, right?

Well, yes, so long as fitting in more words per page does not make the book less readable. There's a sweet spot for optimum words per page. People argue about precisely what that should be, but it's around 12-15 words per line. It's all to do with the frequency and ease with which your eyes move focus to the start of a new line while your brain is still processing the last word of the current line. Once you get beyond about 15 words per page, the ease of reading deteriorates. That's one reason why people find reference works hard to read: because the words per line is often much higher than 15.

So if you are changing your trim size, take care not to move too far outside the words per line range of 12-15.

Can I make hardback books with Createspace?

No.

Createspace rival Lulu does produce hardbacks, and very nice they look too. Some publishers use Createspace for paperbacks and for the ease of getting Amazon to sell them for you, but approach a local or specialist printer for hardback books which they sell directly.

How can I sell to Canada?

The simplest way is to opt for Createspace Expanded Distribution and hope that your paperback will appear a few weeks later at amazon.ca. There are no guarantees that this will happen, but it's always worked for me.

In the world of eBooks, Amazon now has a Kindle store for amazon.ca, meaning that if you publish a Kindle edition of your book through Amazon KDP (Kindle Direct Publishing) then it will automatically be available through amazon.ca

The dominant bookstore in Canada is Indigo. They have a deal with iUniverse who are a vanity publisher. Vanity publishers charge you a lot of money for services you can get cheaper or for free elsewhere, and can tempt naïve authors into believing that a major player in the industry is trying to push their book. So long as you know what you are getting into, and appreciate that there are cheaper alternatives if you go look for them, then there could be some scenarios where vanity presses shouldn't be dismissed out of hand.

The reason I mention iUniverse is because publishing a book though them means that Indigo, Chapters and Coles store managers are allowed to order your book. *Whether any store manager will want to stock your book is another matter entirely!* If you have a significant presence already in Canada as a successful author who is self-publishing new or backlist titles, then publishing through iUniverse could be worth investigating.

There's a general point I make about authors wanting to get wide distribution. Setting up all the possible distribution channels that might take your books can soak up a lot of your time and some money too, and for most self-published authors only leads to sales disappointment. But this is not a once-and-for-all decision. You can, for example, sell just a Kindle eBook and Createspace paperback to begin with (the easiest and bestselling option for eBooks and paperbacks respectively) and get on with writing the next book in your series. Once you have a series of books, some fans and decent sales, got back and think about wider distribution. You can print your paperback with as many printers as you like (unless using a vanity press who will often take away your right to do this). If your series is selling several thousand copies per day in the US, then setting up a distribution arrangement in Canada is going to be much easier, because with a proven track record it makes vastly more sense for distributors and retailers to work with you.

How can I sell to Europe?

It's simply a question of choosing Amazon Europe in the list of channels in your Createspace book project. Your paperback will automatically be listed at European Amazon stores, such as amazon.co.uk, amazon.es, amazon.fr and amazon.de. The UK is the only store where the native language is English, so don't expect many sales elsewhere in Europe if your book is in English.

If I'm not a US citizen, why am I paying US tax?

If you are US-domiciled, Createspace should deduct 30% of your royalties and pay it to the US government as 'witholding tax'. Most countries have a double taxation treaty, which basically means that so long as you can provide evidence that you are a taxpayer in your country, you can be given a tax number by the US tax authorities (the IRS), and when you can provide Createspace with your US tax number, they will stop taking withholding tax.

If you're waiting to get your tax affairs sorted out, you can email Createspace and ask them to keep your royalty payments on hold until you can provide your US tax id. They are used to receiving this request.

Everything I've just written applies also to eBooks you sell through Smashwords and Amazon KDP.

How you get your US tax ID depends on where you live. I wrote up my little adventure and showed the forms I filled in over at my website (www.timctaylor.com) Having met the IRS people in their bombproof bucket in the bowels of the US embassy in London, I can tell you that they are actually very helpful. If I were starting again from scratch, I would simply have rung them up in the first place and asked them to explain what to do. The London US embassy has an online website with all the contact details, and I expect embassies in other countries do too.

Why can't I have spine text?

Createspace says you need a minimum of 100 pages before they will allow you to add text to the spine. They recommend a minimum of 130. There is a margin of error in printing and what they are trying to avoid is having tiny text that doesn't quite hit the spine and drifts off onto the back or front cover.

If you are just below the page count threshold, you could add some blank pages at the end or increase margins or leading to boost you across the minimum page count. Beware of having margins too large so that the interior looks silly.

If you are doing your own covers or commissioning artwork, a spineless paperback cover looks best if it is one wraparound image. If you have separate front and back images stuck together, I advise you to use your graphics package (such as Gimp or Photoshop) to blur the join.

Is it worth selecting Createspace Expanded Distribution?

You can opt your book into the Expanded Distribution service, which lists your book more widely. This free service used to cost $25, but the argument about whether or not to use Expanded Distribution was never about the setup cost.

The problem with Expanded Distribution is that your margins will be a lot lower with books sold through the Expanded Distribution channel. Sales through the Amazon channel will take a 40% cut whether or not you have Expanded Distribution. In other words, the higher cut (60%) is only for those books sold through the Expanded Distribution channel.

However, you must have one list price for all channels. You can't have a higher price for books sold through Expanded Distribution and a lower one for Amazon. The practical effect is that for novels, you will need to set a fairly expensive list price in order to make much money back in royalties. I've listed out some example royalty rates in the previous section [p21].

For the books I publish, I use Expanded Distribution only for books with Canadian authors where I wanted the paperback to be on sale through amazon.ca. Although I have used Expanded Distribution in the past, that's now the only reason I have for doing so. I would rather have a lower retail price.

If you are publishing a non-fiction book and for which you don't feel your market is especially price sensitive, then Expanded Distribution may make a lot more sense.

How can I link my paperback and Kindle edition on Amazon?

If the titles match, it could happen automatically, though it usually takes several days after publishing to take place. If they aren't linked after a few days, log onto Amazon KDP (where you publish your Kindle book; not Createspace) and go to the *Contact Us* section. There's a list of standard queries; one of them is about linking paperback and Kindle editions. Click on this option, supply the ASIN (the serial number Amazon provide for your Kindle book) and the paperback ISBN. Within 48 hours Amazon will have linked the two.

Should I use Createspace to build my Kindle edition?

No! This runs an automated tool that converts your PDF to a Kindle format book. The results are normally awful, although, to be fair, I have encountered a few authors who say they are satisfied with the results. I've encountered many more who have been horrified by the poor quality of the results. Certainly do not even think of using the Createspace automagic Kindle creation option if your book has any of the following: images, table of contents with page numbers, or drop caps.

Amazon has reduced my retail price. Can they do that?

Yes they can (it's in the small print), and this is common. When you sell your Createspace book through the Amazon channel, Amazon takes 40% of the sales revenue remaining for each book, after the printing and distribution costs have been taken off (and you get the other 60%). Sometimes Amazon will put your book on sale. I don't understand the algorithm that decides when to do this, but there are frequent site-wide sales and probably a random element too. Most books get price reduced at some point but Amazon never warns you when they do this or tell you when the price will revert to normal.

The key point is that *Amazon pays for the price reduction out of their margin.* Your royalty is unaffected. As far as you're concerned, Amazon's price reductions are a good thing.

Help! My paperback book is being sold by someone else and for a high price. Are they pirates?

If someone other than Amazon or Createspace, or a major national book chain, is selling your paperback book then it is very unlikely that something sinister is happening. What's happening is that book retailers are picking up your ISBN (which is by design a public reference identifier) and offering your book. If your book is selling very well, they might actually hold some stock. However, it is much more likely that they have worked out your book is print on demand and they will fulfill any orders they take by themselves placing an order with Createspace. In other words, if they take an order, then they will buy your book and when they buy your book, you get paid. Because they need to make a profit, the price they offer your book for is higher than listed at Amazon.

In some cases, these suppliers are operating in regions where Createspace and Amazon do not operate directly, such as Australia.

Since it costs them next to nothing to list your book, these operators will list pretty much every Createspace title.

I know this bothers a lot of authors, but there is nothing illegal here and there's nothing you can do to stop it. Chances are, no one will ever buy your book through these suppliers. Best advice is to ignore them. It's just part of the scenery of publishing.

Part 2 — A typical book-creation workflow

One-page summary: how to self-publish with Createspace • A typical Createspace workflow: DETAIL

There isn't a single route through the publishing process, but here is a typical workflow that I would use if laying out a novel. I'm assuming that the manuscript is complete but not yet laid out. But first a super-quick summary.

One-page Summary: How to Self-publish with Createspace

1. Create a Createspace account and then a project for your book.
2. Format your Word document according to the advice in this book.
3. Save your Word document in PDF format.
4. Upload your PDF to your Createspace book project. This is your paperback book's interior. Use the internal reviewer tool on the Createspace site to view your interior and correct errors.
5. Either upload a PDF image of your paperback cover (minus the barcode, which Createspace adds for you) or use one of the Createspace cover templates to create your cover automatically.
6. Once you're happy with the look of your book, *submit files for review* (a process that typically takes 24 hours). If the Createspace reviewers are happy then order proof copies (which take about a week to arrive if you are in continental USA.).
7. While you're waiting for your proof copies, enter your book description, bio, price and distribution channels into your book project.
8. When you receive your proof copies, take a hard look and not just at the layout. Unless you have had your book professionally copy edited, it is very common for authors to find typos and other errors in the printed edition that they missed when editing their book on screen. In fact, I have seen this so often that it's best for you to assume that your proof copy *will* have errors and set your publishing timetable to accommodate this.
9. If you find errors, correct them and repeat the process. If not, then from your book project in Createspace, approve your book. Your book will be available immediately for the public to buy from Createspace.com. How long it takes to be available on amazon varies, in my experience from half a day to four days. Read the notice Createspace gives you when you authorize publishing and be patient.
10. Congratulations. You have now published your paperback book!

A TYPICAL CREATESPACE WORKFLOW: DETAIL

Set up your Createspace account

Go to Createspace.com and follow the steps online.

If you are not based in the US, you may have to pay 30% WITHHOLDING TAX on your royalties to the US tax authorities, and then pay tax to your country's authorities on what is left over. For most countries, you can avoid this. [See p40 for more details.] It takes time, so if you need to address withholding tax, don't leave this until later.

Register your book with the US Copyright Office

The best time to do this is before your book is published. That way you get maximum protection of your copyright, and are allowed to upload a PDF or other electronic version of your manuscript rather than send physical books. Costs $35. [See p32 for more details.]

Set up dummy projects

Set up dummy projects for your books so you can see how various layout options might look. Rough up options for layout including: font, font size, margins, leading (line height), page color, trim size, chapter spacing, headers and footers. Doesn't matter if the words in your manuscript aren't finished, just get the dummy edition printed up so you can see the possibilities for yourself.

Obviously we don't want our dummy projects to be published by mistake. I always take care never to apply an ISBN to dummy projects.

Organize cover art

You can do this yourself or cover artists are often listed on the copyright page of books, and you can read this using Amazon's 'look inside' facility. Find some covers you like. Get the artist names from Look Inside, then Google the artists to explore commissioning them.

You might come across two names: COVER ARTIST and COVER DESIGNER. The artist will be the person who creates the main image for the front cover. The cover designer will turn that into a format suitable for a paperback cover. Usually the designer will add the text and in some cases design the back cover and spine background.

Createspace provides wizards for automatically creating your book from basic templates. They are okay but rudimentary. If your aim is to produce a book for family and friends, then the templates are good enough. If you want to sell a book to make money, then good cover art is vital. In fact (and I don't say this lightly ☺) good cover art is more important than good layout and formatting for your book's interior.

There are templates that allow you to upload a cover image for the front cover only. Some people use this to insert the image they already have for their eBook edition when later producing a paperback. This is the only use I would consider making of the Createspace templates if you were intending to sell books.

If you're going to produce the cover yourself, use the base template and information Createspace provides here:
https://www.createspace.com/Help/Book/Artwork.do

Finally, if you're commissioning a paperback cover designer, they will normally accept a commission even if you only give an approximate page count. While you are finishing off the book, the artist will create the cover. When you have your finished interior PDF and final pagecount, you tell the artist who will adjust the spine width to account for any changes in the page count.

Don't wait until you've finished the book to engage a cover artist. Good artists will be booked up months in advance.

For more ideas about cover art see this section [p233]

The cover art for this book!

I should have commissioned artwork for the first edition of book you are reading rather than do it myself. But the book is selling well and I'm reluctant to change something that is working. If sales drop, you can be sure that the first thing I will do is commission a new cover.

Choose trim size

I normally choose 6in. x 9in. 5.25 x 8.25 is another popular choice. An_ _g larger than 6 x 9 is going to feel too large for fiction. [See p37 for more on this.]

Create your main Createspace book project

This is what you will use to publish your book. Make sure you get the title correct.

You will notice a subtitle field. This isn't available when publishing the Kindle edition through Amazon KDP. So if your book has a subtitle I suggest embedding it in the main title field as in this example:

> *My Book: a spy thriller for the cybernetic age*

In other words, don't put 'a spy thriller for the cybernetic age' into the subtitle field.

Createspace will ask you about ISBNs early on. You don't need to supply your ISBN until later if you don't want to.

Set correct paragraph and page/section breaks

Some authors, unfortunately, don't know how to tell Microsoft Word where one paragraph ends and another begins. If this is you, then I'm afraid this is a serious problem. Correct it as soon as possible because you will need to make hundreds or thousands of corrections to fix this and the only way to be sure you have made all the corrections is to carefully read your entire book. Missing page breaks is also a problem but much easier to spot.

Part 3 covers this topic in more detail. [see p59]

Set headers and footers

For a novel, I normally set a centered page number for the footer and do not use a header. I count page numbers from the very start of the book, but don't show the footer until after the front matter.

See [p81] for more details.

Set page layout options in Word

I cover this in much more detail in Part 4 of this book [from p73]. Here's a summary:

- Set page size in your Word document to match your trim size.
- Set the following page setup for most average-sized books: **Margins:** Top—0.75", Bottom—0.75", Inside—0.75", Outside—0.5", Gutter—0.13". **Multiple pages:** Mirror margins. **Apply to:** Whole Document.

Set font and paragraph styling

If you intend to publish more than one book, set yourself up a style set [see p137] and apply it now to your new book.

If this is your first self-published book, try this approach:

1. Pick a selection of commercially published paperbacks from your bookshelf and library to see how professionals lay out books. Pick books from your genre for the most part.
2. Read Parts 4-6 of this book.
3. Go back and look again at the commercially published books. Now you should see them in a new light, noticing details such as leading and hyphenation.
4. Copy your Word manuscript and rename it. Then start formatting using a variety of typefaces, font sizes, leading and other options — one set of styling options per chapter. Upload to your dummy project and get proof copies printed. When considering styling options, there is no substitute for opening up a printed book and seeing how it *really* looks.

Set section breaks

Microsoft Word has the concept of dividing up a document into 'Sections'. Not every book requires sections, but most do. You create a new section by placing the cursor at the end of the last paragraph of the preceding section and inserting a section break. You will often use section breaks instead of page breaks.

Typically, you would use section breaks to separate the front matter (copyright page, title page etc.) from the start of your novel's story. If your book is divided into parts then each part would normally be a new section. Often, you would use section breaks to separate chapters too.

Here are some reasons why you might need section breaks.

- Section breaks allow you to set a different header and footer for the first page of the section. If you have a header, then the convention is to not display the header for the first page of a chapter or a part (by 'part' I mean a book divided into part one, part two and so on, such as the book you are reading now).
- Section breaks allow you to force a new section to be on a facing page (also known as odd-numbered or recto page). Your contents page should start on a facing page, so too should new parts and, optionally, new chapters too. If Word works out that it needs to insert a blank page in order to start the new page on a facing page then it will do so automatically (although you won't see this blank page unless you print or export to PDF). This blank page is more than just a convenience because these blank pages will follow the standard book convention of having neither a footer nor a header. In Microsoft Word, using section breaks *is the only way to achieve this*.
- If you style your heading paragraphs (such as chapter headings) to have 'space above' so that the heading is set some way down from the top of the page, you may find that Word ignores this blank space when your heading is at the top of a page after a page break. You can fix this by inserting a blank paragraph in normal style above the heading, and in some versions of Word (prior to 2013), you can hunt around in the accessibility section of Word Options and turn off the option to 'suppress blank space at the top of the page'. But the simplest approach is to use section breaks. Word will honor the spacing you set for a paragraph immediately following a section break, but will often ignore your spacing for a paragraph following a page break.

See [p89] for more on sections.

Consider use of ornaments

By ornaments, I mean graphical flourishes, fancy lines, icons and so forth, often used in headers, titles and scene breaks, such as…

They can add a touch of class, they can break up blocks of dry text in non-fiction, and they can look ridiculous if you overdo it.

Set front and back matter

Front matter is all the material that goes before the main text of your book starts. This includes, title, half title, copyright, dedication and (where appropriate) a contents page. [I have examples of front matter from p196].

Back matter is – you guessed it – what goes after the main body. Some books don't have any back matter at all, but I advise you to use an 'About the Author' section and a link to some of your other books. Some books have a sample of the sequel or companion book. Don't overdo it, though. Books that have endless adverts at the end don't go down well with readers.

Curl your quotes

All your quotes should be curled.

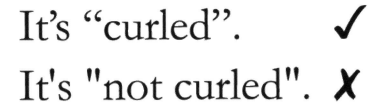

You should be able to see the difference between the two. The 'uncurled' version was invented for use with typewriters and made sense to be used with the limited character sets of early computers. Books have always used curled quotes and apostrophes. So should yours.

Setting curled quotes starts with setting an option in Word Options and automatically replacing your existing text. However, it isn't as simple as this. See [p188] for more details on how to do this right.

Perform other final checks

Get your ellipses consistent. Clear away double spaces and spaces at the start of lines. [There's a list of tasks in the section on Final Checks on p187.]

Upload paperback interior

From the book project section of Createspace, go to INTERIOR and upload the file for your book's interior. I always create the image of my paperback interior in the PDF format because that gives me more control and consistency. I use a printer driver from Adobe to 'print' from my Word docx file into a file in PDF format. I upload this to my Createspace project.

You can also upload your book in other formats: doc, docx, and rtf. They may work for you, but there could be a higher likelihood of problems. See DO I REALLY NEED TO UPLOAD A PDF on p191.

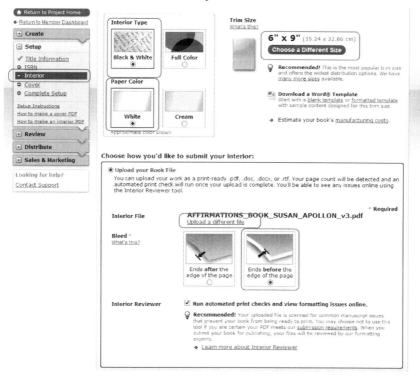

Figure 2: Uploading to Createspace

The various settings you should use when uploading your PDF interior (or other file format) depend on what you want to do. Unless you want images extending to the edge of the page (which is an advanced special effect) you should set bleed to 'Ends before the edge of the page' as in the screenshot above.

Check results in Interior Reviewer

When you upload your interior, wait a few minutes for the Createspace site to run automated checks, and then you will be shown the INTERIOR REVIEWER. This lists the errors and warnings found in the automated checks. You can also skip through the pages in a mockup of how they would appear in the printed book. It's not speedy, but you should take the time to run through every page. Pay particular attention to:

Is the header and footer correct for every page? Do not assume that just because the first few hundred pages are correct, that the next page will be. A large book can have several hundred *separate* header and footer definitions! [See HEADERS AND FOOTERS on p81].

Is each image placed where you expect? [See Part5 — Images on p141].

Where you want pages to appear on facing/ odd-numbered/ recto pages, are they appearing in the right place? [See SECTIONS on p89].

Upload Cover

You can either upload a cover as a PDF file, or you can use the cover creator tool from Createspace. This book is primarily about formatting the interior, but I've plenty of experience working with cover artists, which I've shared in the topic on COVER ART TIPS on [p233].

Print proof/ beta copies

Always order a proof copy from the Review | Proof Your Book section of your book project on Createspace. It is very common for problems to be apparent in the printed version that mysteriously pass you by when you look at your book onscreen. Check for all the formatting issues page by page (in particular, headers and footers) but I thoroughly recommend you actually read the book cover to cover. Get friends and family to read copies too (you can order several proofs at a time). Clearly, all this takes time, so budget that time into your timetable from the beginning.

If you aren't a US resident, then you have a potential problem here. Createspace prints proofs in the US, so shipping times might run to weeks. I'm based in the UK. Sometimes I use another printer (such as Lulu) to produce private beta and review copies, while I'm waiting for my Createspace proofs to arrive. However, you cannot use books printed by another printer as a reliable means to proof books printed by Createspace.

Finalize book description

The book description you enter as part of your Createspace book project will eventually appear in your book's page on Amazon and other retailers. Work hard to get this right. Try making several versions and try them out on friends and colleagues.

Run your beta-reader program

It's a good idea to involve friends and followers and fellow authors as BETA READERS. Good beta readers involved early enough can steer the development of the book. Later on and it's very expensive to fundamentally change your book but many pairs of eyes will spot typos and logic errors that somehow slipped past your best editing efforts.

Something I often do to reward beta readers with my Greyhart Press imprint is to list them prominently at the beginning of the book and send them a complimentary copy of the paperback with my thanks. Many people have written to tell me how they appreciate this.

Create your eBook version

At present there are two main eBook formats: Kindle format (for Kindles) and ePUB format (for everything else). Each comes with different versions and subtle variations. There are other formats too, such as Microsoft Reader, PDF, and interactive iOS or Android apps, but for the majority of self-publishers these are an irrelevance except possibly the PDF which you can generate from Microsoft Word anyway.

There are many ways to build your eBook. Createspace offers an automated Kindle book generation service, and that would seem initially to be the best approach since you're using Createspace anyway. I have known authors (usually novelists) with simple requirements and limited expectations who are satisfied with the results. However, they are outnumbered by authors who have been disappointed with their results. And this service is automated. For example, if you are writing non-fiction then you almost certainly need a table of contents. The Createspace auto-generated Kindle book will include the same table of contents with page numbers that no longer make sense and without preserving the spacing between contents entry and page number. It looks awful, and worst of all, this will be visible if anyone 'Looks Inside' your Kindle edition on Amazon.

Self-publishers can get heated and very partisan in their support for one approach to constructing eBooks over the others. Unfortunately, a significant percentage of what you can read online about eBook design is inaccurate or incomplete.

I have listed some references on eBook design [p270] for how you might build your own eBook.

Alternatively, pay someone to build your book for you. There are some excellent eBook designers, and many who will try to con you out of your money but don't know enough to build you a book that will be robust across many platforms. Most fit somewhere in between. Word of mouth is the best way to find eBook designers. Or you can 'Look Inside' Kindle books on Amazon.com that look good and search for the name of the eBook designer in the copyright page.

Part 3 — Formatting: Setting correct paragraph and page breaks

Writing robust paragraphs • Manual line feed • How to set page breaks • How to fix badly marked paragraphs

Writing Robust Paragraphs

The most fundamental task of a word processor is to wrap lines for you automatically.

If you look at this book, you will see it consists for the most part of paragraphs, each of which is separated from the next by a small gap. Most paragraphs have more than one line of words. In fact, you are reading such a paragraph now.

When you type such a paragraph into Microsoft Word, the correct approach is to keep on typing until you get to the end of the paragraph. Then you tell Word that you've finished the paragraph by pressing the Enter key. Then you start typing the next paragraph.

> For simplicity I'm using the term 'Enter key'. You might refer to it as 'Return' or 'Carriage return/ line feed'. The button on my keyboard has a short downward line followed by a longer line to the left that terminates in an arrow. These are all names for the same button. Full-sized keyboards with a numeric keypad will have an Enter key as well as a Return key. It is very rare for PC/Windows software to distinguish between them, but some Mac software does, including Word, as we will see in a moment with 'manual line feeds'.

You must not tap the Enter key until you have finished the paragraph. Inside a paragraph, it is the word processor's responsibility to automatically decide when a line has finished and so therefore it needs to start the next word on a new line. If you try to do this *yourself* by hitting the Enter key in the middle of a paragraph, then you are going to have a badly formatted paperback book. And if you use the same Word manuscript as the basis of your eBook edition, that is likely to be even worse. In the latter case, I'm not talking 'doesn't quite look professionally formatted', I mean 'utterly unreadable, ask for money back and complain about poor quality to Amazon.'

The reason is simple. You might think you are setting a new line at the correct place. But it is dependent upon variables such as font size, margins and page size. As soon as any of these variables change, your new line *will be in the wrong place*. And with eBooks, all of these variables are completely out of your control.

Let me show you. I'm going to repeat the previous paragraph with identical font size, margins and everything else except I will change the typeface.

The reason is simple. You might think you are setting a new line at the correct place. But it is dependent upon font size, margins and page size. As soon as any of these variables change, your new line will be in the wrong place. And with eBooks, all of these variables are completely out of your control.

You should see the lines wrapping at a slightly different place. Now I'm going to press the Enter key where the lines ended in the original example. In other words, this would have looked right in the original layout, but as soon as I change the font, look what happens...

The reason is simple. You might think you are setting a new line at the

correct place. But it is dependent upon font size, margins and page size.

As soon as any of these variables change, your new line will be in the

wrong place. And with eBooks, all of these variables are completely out

of your control.

The screenshot below shows how your document *should* look.

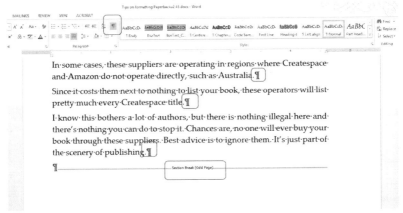

Figure 3: How your paragraphs should look

Notice in the Ribbon that I've ringed the show/hide button (¶). Setting show/hide on means that I see a paragraph mark at the end of each paragraph and a section break at the end of the page.

The 'show/hide' or 'paragraph mark' (¶) is properly called a 'pilcrow'. To insert it into the text of this book, I've used 'Insert Character' from the Ribbon and picked the 'Arial Unicode MS' character set and gone hunting for the pilcrow. If you are reading the eBook version, you won't have the Arial Unicode MS font installed on your reader, but through the magic of Unicode, if your eBook reader has any font that includes the pilcrow, then your reader should be able to display the character. Modern eBook devices and tablets have good enough Unicode support to display pilcrows and many thousands of characters beyond, although current Kobo readers aren't able to use fallback fonts in this way.

Now we'll see the same text but with the paragraphs broken up. Here I've hit the Enter key at the end of each line instead of at the end of each paragraph. Remember, if we turned off the show/hide option (and so hide the pilcrows) both examples would initially look identical. But if we changed page size, margins, font, font size or even potentially our version of Word, the lines would break in the wrong place in the second example but would adjust automatically in the first.

In·some·cases,·these·suppliers·are·operating·in·regions·where·Createspace·¶
and·Amazon·do·not·operate·directly,·such·as·Australia.¶
¶
Since·it·costs·them·next·to·nothing·to·list·your·book,·these·operators·will·list¶
pretty·much·every·Createspace·title.¶
¶
I·know·this·bothers·a·lot·of·authors,·but·there·is·nothing·illegal·here·and¶
there's·nothing·you·can·do·to·stop·it.·Chances·are,·no·one·will·ever·buy·your¶
book·through·these·suppliers.·Best·advice·is·to·ignore·them.·It's·just·part·of¶
the·scenery·of·publishing.¶
¶
¶
¶
¶

Figure 4: How your paragraphs should NOT look!

Pilcrows don't always look the same, but any differences are cosmetic. The most obvious difference is that sometimes the head is filled in and sometimes not. In the screenshot above, the text uses a font called Palatino Linotype, and for that font the pilcrows are hollow. At the bottom I've added three blank lines in another font: Calibri, for which the pilcrow is filled in.

So far I've written about using the Enter key before the end of the paragraph. Sometimes people keep pressing the space bar or the tab key for the same effect. This has the same results and causes the same formatting disasters as soon as any of the variables changes (such as font size or margins).

Manual line feed.

For completeness, I need to mention the MANUAL LINE FEED. You can type in a manual line feed in Word for Windows by pressing the SHIFT and Enter key at the same time. For Mac you need Shift+Return (Shift+Enter adds a page break). This is a legitimate way of telling Word that you want a new line but you do not want to start a new paragraph.

People do this sometimes in order to start a new line but avoiding the styling for a new paragraph (such as the 'space before' the new paragraph or the 'first line indent'). Usually this is for titles or for poetry. You can use styles for the same effect but a manual line feed can sometimes be a little quicker.

The key thing about manual line feeds for paperback books is that you use them only for special effects and not to take away your word processor's job of wrapping lines of body text. If you do, you will get the same problem of lines breaking at the wrong place that we've seen earlier in this section.

Take care if using manual line feeds in eBooks in order to generate blank lines. Some eReaders will ignore your blank lines; it all depends on how you go from Word document to eBook and what you are using to read the book. If the html code inside your book has blank lines like this:

```
<p> <br/> </p>
```

Then your blank lines will be ignored by some eReaders.

What you want for blank lines is this:

```
<p>   </p>
```

How to set page breaks correctly

Just as you need to know how to tell Word when to start a new paragraph, the same is true of telling Word when to start a new page. Leave Word to decide when to start a new page except where you want to force a page break.

For example, in your novel you will probably want to start each chapter on a new page, but within each chapter, leave Word to decide when to start a new page.

Some authors try to force a new page by hitting the Enter key until the cursor moves to the next page. Don't do this! There's a high chance that the line you want to start at the top of the new page will appear in the wrong place in the final edition of your paperback. For your eBook, it is an absolute certainty.

The correct way to do this is to move the cursor to the end of page and then insert a PAGE BREAK or a SECTION BREAK.

Although you can use the Ribbon to insert page breaks (from the left of the INSERT menu), it's such a common thing to do that I use the key shortcut. On a Windows keyboard hold down the Alt key and 'I' simultaneously. Release and then press 'b'. [For Mac, use SHIFT + ENTER]

At the end of the page before you force a page break, you should see the following:

- The last word of the last sentence of the page (usually terminated by a period).
- Then you need a paragraph break (by hitting the Enter key)

- Then you need the page break (Alt+I, B or using the Ribbon)

If you miss off the paragraph break you can get some very strange results, because the first line of the next page will be part of the same paragraph as the end of the preceding page. That can confuse Word!

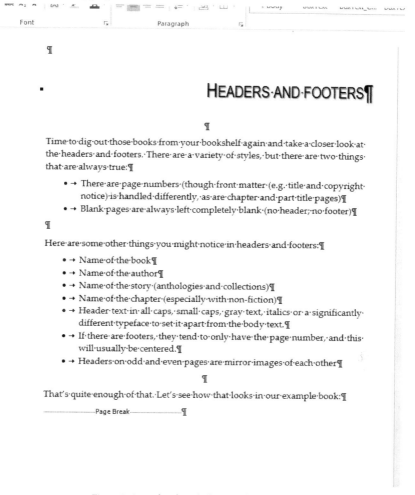

Figure 5: A page break at the bottom of the page

If this has been new for you, then congratulations, because you've just learned some crucial techniques! Have a play with them now with a new document in Word until you are comfortable setting paragraph and page breaks and in turning show/hide on and off.

. badly marked paragraphs

ormatting techniques in this book can be applied at the end of the book-writing process, typically as you get to the final editing stages. Correctly marking paragraphs is different. If you aren't in the habit of marking paragraphs correctly, stop whatever you are doing, learn the technique and apply it immediately.

Try to solve the problem now of badly formatted paragraphs by correcting your manuscript up to this point. You probably won't catch every instance, so fix the majority now, and keep an eye out for any that remain lurking as you proceed through the writing and editing of your book.

In the box below I have described an advanced technique for automatically detecting some badly marked paragraphs, but an initial pass, try this:

1. Change your View to Web Layout (on the Ribbon — View | Document Views)
2. Decrease the font size. Don't change the font formatting. Instead, change the view zoom, by adjusting the +/- slider at the bottom right of the screen to a smaller percentage.
3. Turn show/hide to 'show'. (On the Ribbon — Home | Paragraph | Click the Pilcrow (that looks like a filled-in 'P' pointing backwards).
4. Now you should be able to spot bad paragraph breaks more easily. In particular, look for lines that start with a lower case letter.

Don't expect to catch every problem in one pass. Have a go, let your brain rest, and then try again in a few days. When you get your proof copies of your paperback, look again for lines that don't start with the right word.

Fixing badly marked paragraphs is a problem I face as a professional book designer. I'll share a technique I use to catch many falsely broken paragraphs, though this is an advanced technique.

Copy the text from Word into a text editor with RegEx capability, such as Notepad++

First, do a RegEx search and replace to remove blank space from the start of paragraphs.

Search for the following expression...

$$^+$$

And replace with *nothing* (in other words, make sure the replace box is completely empty)

Then search for the following regular expression with case sensitivity set on:

$$^[a-z]$$

That expression means 'find paragraphs that start with a lower case alphabetic character'. A few instances will be valid, but most will be caused by a paragraph being broken when it shouldn't be.

Part 4 — Formatting: Page Layout

Layout strategy • Copying page setup from a template • Headers & Footers • Link to previous • Sections • Smashwords, Kindles, and sections • Page numbers • Introducing styles • Justification • Paragraph indentation • Paragraph spacing • A starting set of styles • Fonts and typefaces • Leading • Super style sets

PLAN THE LAYOUT STRATEGY FOR YOUR PAGES

Take a selection of professionally produced printed books off your shelves, and have a look at how they're laid out. Then come back to me.

Ready?

If you were looking at adult fiction books then you should have found some variation, but a typical approach works like this:

- The title at the beginning of the book is on a **facing** page. In word processors, these are called **odd** pages. Why? Because the facing pages always have the odd page numbers. Go on, try it. All the books on your shelf will work that way. (In publishing we sometimes call odd pages 'recto' pages, and even 'verso').

- If you have **Parts** in your book (this book is divided into Part 1, Part 2, and Part 3 and so on) then they will be on odd pages, and the chapter heading that follows will also be on an odd page.

- This means you will always get a blank page between the odd page with the Part heading and the odd page with the chapter heading. Depending on your other page layout choices, you may get other blank pages too.

- Blank pages have no header and no footer. They are totally blank. They still count in the page count but the page number is not displayed.

- Pages with chapter headings don't have a header. They might have a footer. Some books don't have footers, only a header, and for these books, pages with chapter headings do not display a page number.

- Some books always start a chapter on an odd page, others don't. If the book is a collection or anthology of short stories, then new stories should definitely start on odd pages.

- Some books start the first line of a chapter with a drop cap. Some books format the first few words of a chapter in small caps instead of or as well as the drop cap.

Let's look at some examples from our sample book, *Drift*. Here are a couple of screenshots from the Interior Reviewer, a great tool Createspace provides as part of your book project for inspecting how your book will look.

Figure 6: A new part

The first example is mostly white space. Not very interesting, you might think, but in book formatting, we want blank pages to really be blank, no headers here. Same with the Part title. Ultimately, the blank page and the lack of headers in this example has come about from the way I defined the sections in Microsoft Word. The blank page was added automatically (because I set section start to *odd page*, and *different first page* for the header. See the Sections topic [p89]). To some people familiar with books (such as those reviewers you were thinking of sending a copy to) missing off the blank page, or having a header over the Part title page looks amateurish. Don't give them a reason to think poorly of your book!

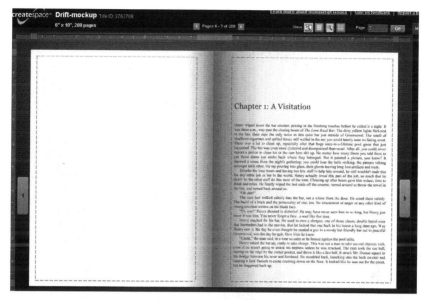

Figure 7: Chapter starting on facing page

In this next screenshot, we've turned the page. There is a blank page added automatically because we want the first chapter of a new Part to start on a facing page.

You're possibly thinking at this point that I didn't actually bother with headers at all. Honestly, I did put in a header, and if you turned the page to read on into chapter1, then you would see them.

We'll look in more detail at headers and footers — and their connection to sections — shortly. But first, we need to look at page setup and how to use templates provided by Createspace and the other print-on-demand sites.

COPY THE PAGE SETUP FROM THE CREATESPACE TEMPLATE INTO YOUR DOCUMENT

Lulu and Createspace have Microsoft Word templates for each TRIM SIZE (trim size is the page size of your book, for example 6" x 9" is common). If you've already written your manuscript in Word, do you copy into the template or copy the template definition into your manuscript? What if you aren't using Word at all?

My answer to both questions is to examine the page setup for the template and apply the page layout settings to your manuscript file in Word. The alternative is to copy your manuscript into the template chapter by chapter. I don't like the second approach because it looks dangerous. (How can you be sure you've copied all the right pages into the right place in the right order? Answer: you can't without a thorough read through.) Also, pasting tends to bring across more than you think (such as page setups and styles) and overwrite what was in the template (which defeats its purpose).

I'm going to show you the page setup I used for the *Drift* manuscript at Createspace. The terms (such as gutters) are standard, so even if you aren't using Word, you should have similar options available to you. If you aren't sure what the terms mean, look at your manual or Google. (Hint: Microsoft Word help is online [see p270] so you don't even need to use Word to read its manual or see a huge amount of online guidance).

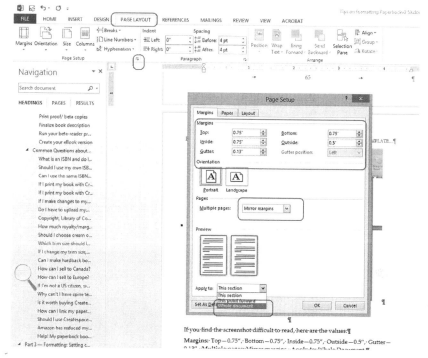

Figure 8: Page setup — margins

If you find the screenshot difficult to read, here are the values:

Margins: Top—0.75", Bottom—0.75", Inside—0.75", Outside—0.5", Gutter—0.13". **Multiple pages:** Mirror margins. **Apply to:** Whole Document.

You should be entering all these values, but I've highlighted a few I'm going to talk about.

To bring up the 'Page Setup' window in Word 2007, 2010 & 2013, click the little box on the bottom-right of the Page Layout section of the Ribbon.

Mirror margins: This is a key setting. It tells Word that the page layout here is for facing (odd-numbered) pages. Whatever you set here will also be used for even-numbered pages, but the margins will be a mirror image. In this example, the margin is set much larger at the inside of the page (the bit that disappears into the middle and is glued to the binding).

Margins and gutter: To begin with, I suggest using these values because they're what Createspace uses in the templates they provide. If you're producing a standard paperback novel of around 200-400 pages then these settings will suit you fine. [We'll cover more options for margins and gutters later at p236].

Apply To: Apply the settings to your entire document. Normally the pages will all be the same. The differences will be with headers and footers, which we'll see later.

A note on screenshots and Word versions

The screenshot we've just seen is from Word 2013. If you have Word 2007 or 2010, then your Ribbon will look slightly differently. Don't worry! Any differences here are minor. Elsewhere in the book if there are important differences between Word editions, I will point them out in the text.

Figure 9: Set page size to match trim size

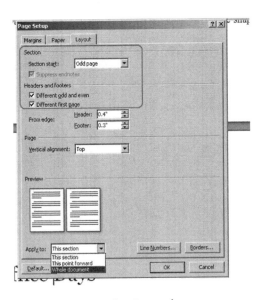

Figure 10: Page Setup — layout

Remember in the last topic, I mentioned that we want certain pages to ﬞ .vays appear on an odd-numbered page? For example, when you begin a new Part, or a new story in an anthology, you want the title page for the Part/ story to be on an odd page. That's what we're telling Word to do by saying **Section start: Odd page**. When you print the document, or convert to PDF, Word will insert a blank page between sections if it needs to in order to start the new section with an odd page. You won't see this blank page in Word even in print layout, but it will be created when you print or create the PDF.

In the example I'm working through (*Drift* by Andrew Cyrus Hudson, a typically formatted fiction book) you will want different headers and footers for odd and even pages and a different first page.

Apply this to the entire document, though you might want to change the section start setting later on. If you have decided you don't want to insist that new chapters start on odd pages, instead of setting Section start to odd page, you should set **next page** as your default. If you decide that you have a few sections that you do want to start with an odd page (perhaps for each Part of the book) but want your chapter-heading pages to start wherever they fall, then that's not a problem because you can define how each section should start independently of the default. (There is a topic later about sections — p89 —and how to set properties for sections).

The Createspace templates are currently here[1]; Lulu's are here[2]. I think it is worth looking at both sites for community help, templates, wizards and such like.

I'll weigh the pros and cons of Lulu and Createspace in Part 7, but one thing worth pointing out now is that they are all changing and improving over time. So if it's been a while since you last produced a book, it's worth looking at the other site because their tools, guidance, and pricing might have moved on since you last looked. For example, when I wrote the first edition of this book, Createspace had not set up operations in the UK. Now Createspace books are printed in the UK for UK retail customers (typically, those bought through amazon.co.uk) although, unfortunately proof copies and author-purchased copies are still printed in the USA and shipped across the Atlantic. Still, that's a major difference for British authors and a good example of why you should

---

[1] **Createspace:** https://www.createspace.com/Products/Book/InteriorPDF.jsp
[2] **Lulu** http://www.lulu.com/uk/publish/books/

keep your eyes open for changes, perhaps by subscribing to a few blogs that cover book publishing and book layout.

Headers and Footers

Time to dig out those books from your bookshelf again and take a closer look at the headers and footers. There are a variety of styles, but there are two things that are always true:

- There are always page numbers, although front matter (e.g. title and copyright notice) is often handled differently.
- Blank pages are always left completely blank (no header; no footer)

Here are some other things you might notice in headers and footers:

- Name of the book
- Name of the author
- Name of the story (anthologies and collections)
- Name of the chapter (especially with non-fiction)
- Header text in all caps, small caps, gray text, italics or a significantly different typeface to set it apart from the body text.
- If there are footers, they tend to only have the page number, and this will usually be centered.
- Headers on odd and even pages are mirror images of each other, by which I mean that if the header is aligned toward the outer edge of the page, on an odd-numbered page they will be aligned right, and aligned left on an even-numbered page.

That's quite enough of that. Let's see how that looks in our example book:

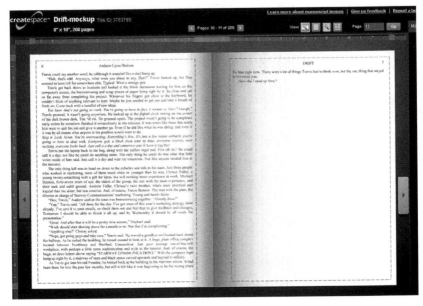

Figure 11: Body text example

Here, on pages 6 and 7, we are past the title pages and blank pages we saw earlier, and showing how the main body of the book works. I've taken a standard style of mirrored headers with no footer. Although the headers are mirrored (the page number is always towards the outer edge of the page) the text is not the same. Even pages have the author name, and odd pages have the book title.

I have placed the title in all caps, using the same font as the body text. Because the author's name is fairly lengthy, I decided to keep Andrew Cyrus Hudson in mixed case. Your headers should recede into the background as the reader reads the story, and I judged that this was best served here by using mixed case. It was a close call; keeping all caps or small caps would have helped differentiate the title from the body text. I tried both and thought this looked best.

And that's what you should do, too. Read the advice, look at a sample of books, and then experiment to see what works best.

Before we see how we deliver this in Word, I'll turn the page once more in Createspace's Interior Reviewer tool.

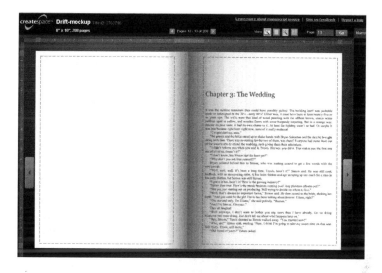

We've seen this screenshot in earlier tips, but it's a timely reminder that in my page layout plan, I decided to set each chapter so it started on an odd (facing) page. When that means a blank page is needed (as here) it should have no header and no footer. The first page of a chapter has no header either. Note that in *Drift* I'm not using footers. If I were (probably with a centered page number) then the first page of the chapter **would** have the footer and the blank page **would not**.

Okay, that's quite enough of Createspace for a few moments, let's look at how we set this up in Word.

The first thing you need to know about Word is that in order to format a print book divided into chapters or similar, you need to divide up your Word document into *sections*. We'll do exactly that in the next tip, but with regard to headers and footers, the important things about sections are:

- For each section, you can choose new headers/footers, or carry on the same as the last section.
- For page numbers, you can choose to carry on counting from where you left off last section, or restart at a new number (which you would do if you wanted Roman page numbers for your front matter (usually i, ii, iii rather than 1, 2, 3)
- You can define headers/footers to be different for the first page of a section. That's how we stop the header appearing on the first page of a chapter or part.

83

Now, let's see some screenshots of this in Microsoft Word 2007. If you have an earlier version of Word, don't worry. Word 2007 introduced the Ribbon, which makes the user experience very different. However, all the facilities I'm about to explain about were there in earlier versions, and so you can learn the concepts and then look at the online help to explain how to access them in your version of Word.

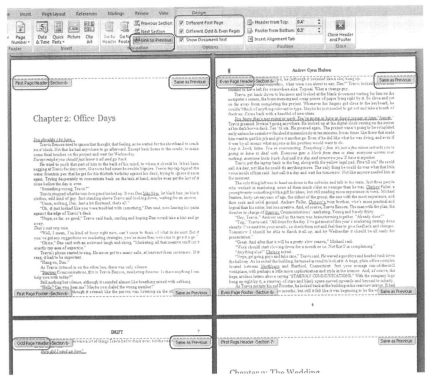

Figure 12: Headers & footers in Word 2007/10/13

Here we have pages 5, 6, 7, and 8. These pages in Word define what you saw earlier in the Createspace Interior Reviewer. I have clicked in the header area (i.e. the top of the page) to bring up the header and footer tools. This has grayed the main document text, brought up a new menu in the Ribbon (Header & Footer Design), and added the pale blue tabs, which give you vital information about how you have defined your sections.

[This is the busiest image in the book. If you are struggling to follow the screenshot is available on my website (www.timctaylor.com) or (far better), c Microsoft Word and follow the steps to bring up a similar display on your compu _r.]

We'll start with the blue tabs (the ones that say 'First Page Header – Section 6 – ', 'Odd Page Header...' or 'Even Page header...'). You can see that pages 5, 6 & 7 are section 6, and page 8 kicks off section 7. What you can't see is that page 4 was the last page of section 5, and that I currently have section 6 selected (because my cursor was in chapter two when I brought up the header tools. You can move between sections by clicking next/previous section in the Ribbon).

Now look at the areas I've ringed in red. On the Ribbon, I have set the following options that I'm interested in right now:

- Different first page
- Different odd and even pages

And now look at the red rings over the pages (you'll just have to imagine them if you're watching in black-and-white; best to open up this screen in Word or on my website). I've ringed three of those pale-blue 'tabs'. They read 'First page header', 'even page header', 'odd page header'. This means that section 6 has three different headers, which is precisely what we told it to do as we've just seen on the Ribbon.

We only have three pages for this chapter. If we had more, then any following pages would alternate between even page header and odd page header.

To set what goes into the header — in other words, the page number and the title/ author — first of all I have to pick the correct header. If I want to set the odd page header, for example, I need to click the page where the pale-blue tab says 'odd page header'. That will set the header for all the odd pages in the current section.

Next, I click on the header button in the Ribbon like this...

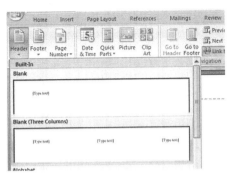

Figure 13: The header button in Word 2007/10/13

Here, I've picked the option for 'Blank (Three Columns)'. To carry on with the odd page header example, I:

- Clicked on the central '[Type text]' and replaced with 'DRIFT'

- Deleted the left-hand '[Type text]'

- Clicked on the right-hand '[Type text]' and entered the page number. Now, in this case I clicked on **Page Number** and selected **Current Position**. Page numbers can be tricky (especially with Word 2003), so we'll come back to them in their own tip — p94 — once we've dealt with the rest of headers and sections.

We define the even page header in the same way, but with different text and placement.

As for the first page header... Well, I don't want the first page of the section to have *any* header, so I leave it blank.

If you're going mad trying to bring up the Header & Footer Tools...

The simplest way to bring up the Header & Footer Tools in the Ribbon is to double-click the header or footer part of the page in Print View. If this doesn't seem to work, try double-clicking at the *very top of the page*, above the header (or the very bottom for the footer).

Link to previous

If you look at the last couple of screenshots you'll see a Ribbon option . called 'Link to previous' and in the pale-blue tabs it says 'same as previous'. You need to know how to use this.

Suppose you have 100 chapters, and you want the odd and even headers that I used in *Drift*. You also want to leave off the header on the first page of a chapter.

That means you must have 100 sections.

Each section must have a separate first page, odd page, and even page header.

That's 300 headers. You really don't want to define each one by hand; you want to define each one just once, right? For that you need 'link to previous'.

- Start towards the **beginning** of your document, at the first place you want to start using the standard headers (i.e. after the front matter).

- Define all three of your headers.

- For each subsequent section, instead of defining three new headers, click on the 'link to previous' Ribbon button **for each heading type** and it will inherit what you defined in the previous section **for that heading type**. (When I say 'heading type', I mean one of odd- / even-/ first-page header).

- Continue this all the way through to the end.

An added bonus, is that this means you can alter something about the header (perhaps set to all caps) and the change will be reflected in all the linked headers.

One gotcha here is that the 'next section' / 'previous section' buttons on the Ribbon don't work quite the way you might think. It's best explained with an example.

Consider Chapter 2 that we saw a couple of screenshots ago. Suppose we start off on the first page of section 6 (remember — we've defined section 6 to mean the same as Chapter 2). If we click 'Next section', you would be forgiven for thinking we would move from section 6 to section 7. We don't! We move from 'First page header - Section 6' to 'Even page header - Section 6'.

If we carried on hitting 'Next section' we would then get 'Odd page header - section 6'; then 'First page header - section 7', 'Even page header - Section 7' and so on.

I'm trying to explain in writing here, but this would be a good point for you to go, define some headings, and play with the buttons to see how they work.

Which, what, huh?

I used to find it confusing to work out which setting affected which part of the book. So here's a summary.

- We divide the book into **sections**.
- Some things are **properties of a section**, such as whether we have a different first page header and some settings we'll see in the page numbers tip [p94].
- We have up to **three different header definitions for each section**. The next/previous buttons move between these headers and not between sections, despite what the name says.
- We can save a whole lot of effort (and risk) by making our header definitions inherit from the previous section using Word's *Link to Previous* setting.

As for footers, they work the same way as headers.

We're done for this topic. In the next few topics we'll be looking a little more at sections and page numbers, but we've got most of it done in the section you've just read.

SECTIONS

We've seen a lot about sections in the past few tips, so let's finish the job now. In the book you're reading, we're looking at using Microsoft Word to layout books to send to a printer, such as Createspace. In that context there are really only two reasons for using sections:

1. To allow us to set headers and footers
2. To auto-generate blank pages if we want chapters or Parts to begin on an odd-numbered page.

In other words, we need to put in sections to make possible the book layout plan we set out earlier [p73].

Before we jump in and start creating sections, I'll add two more things:

- **Smashwords** — you might also want eBook editions of your book published through Smashwords. Current Smashwords guidelines say you shouldn't use section breaks; I've just told you that you must use section breaks! At the end of this tip, I'll give some Smashwords-specific tips.
- **Changing margins** — Word does give you the option to choose different margins for each section. I would avoid doing that for book layouts for reasons of simplicity and robustness. If you really wanted to play with variable margins then that's up to you.

What's a section?

Sections are a way of breaking your document into chunks, well... okay, sections. There are two things you need to know:

1. Each section can be given its own value for a set of attributes. The attributes of most interest to us are: header & footer definition, section start property (whether the section has to start on a facing page), page number format, and the page number to start counting from.

2. We can set the first page of the section to have a different header/footer, and we can force the first page of the section to start on a facing (odd-numbered) page. According to the book layout approach we're following, that means we need to start a new section for every Part and for every chapter.

To insert a break in Word 2007 and later, you can do so through the Ribbon as follows:

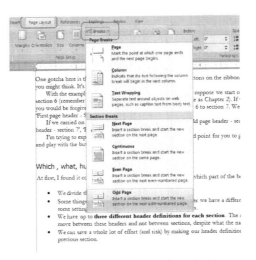

Figure 14: Adding breaks in Word 2007/10/13

Here I've selected the section break that corresponds to the **odd page section start**. We use this to begin a new part or new chapter on a facing (odd) page, telling Word to insert a blank page if it needs to.

Let's suppose you are at the end of Part 2 of your book and want to start on Part 3. On the last page of Part 2, insert an odd page section break and then add your Part 3 title text to the next page. With Word you won't see any blank pages until you print them or (very important, this) you create the PDF. Don't forget to test your PDF to check blank pages are inserted at the right point.

If, on the other hand, you are coming up to a new chapter, but you *don't* want to force it to begin on a facing page, then you insert a section break with a **next page section start**.

If you have an older version of Word, or you want a faster way to insert breaks quickly, you can use the keyboard shortcut 'ALT+I', followed by 'B'

This brings up the following dialog:

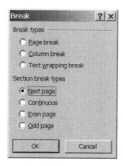

Figure 15: Word 2003 breaks

This does exactly the same as the Ribbon dialog.

Have a play creating section breaks with a backed-up document. Then bring up the **Page Layout | Page Setup** dialog we saw earlier:

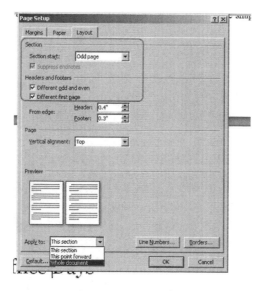

Figure 16: Page Setup dialog

All the settings on all the tabs of this dialog are properties of each section. You can set different values for each section if you wanted to. But you don't want to, so don't do it.

Pay close attention to the **section start** value in this dialog. This setting tells you the type of section break between the preceding section and the current one. So, if you are in section 2, and the Page Setup dialog says: *Section start: Odd page*, then that means the break between sections 1 and 2 is of the odd page type. The Page Setup dialog tells you nothing about any section breaks between this section and the *next* one.

I've come across confusing behavior with section break types where you *already have sections defined*, and you subsequently try to change the section type. In my case I tried deleting a section break in print layout view and then adding a new one of a different type. My change reverted back to the old section type when I wasn't looking. Most mysterious!

If that happens, look at the **section start** settings. Your inserted section break will probably be reverting to the section start value of the *following* section, in which case change the setting in the page setup dialog first, and then insert your section break.

There's some general guidance from Microsoft on sections online.[3]

Smashwords, Kindle editions, ePub and section breaks

This only applies if you want to create eBooks, especially if you upload a Word doc to Smashwords. The Smashwords style guide (which you would be wise to follow) says you shouldn't use section breaks (although authors have reported to me that they have used section breaks without any problems for Smashwords). I've told you that you must use section breaks for the print layout. Also, if you are creating a Kindle edition yourself (i.e. not through Smashwords) then that will accept section breaks with no problem.

When I create books, I often create a Kindle, ePub, Smashwords, and print edition. My approach is to keep to a single version for as long as possible and then break out into giving each version its tweaks at the last moment. [Using **Style Sets** makes this much easier... See p137].

So for a more general approach for managing multi-edition documents, here's what I do:

---

[3]   http://office.microsoft.com/en-us/word-help/change-the-layout-or-formatting-in-one-section-of-your-document-HP001226502.aspx

- Write, tidy, edit your document in print layout as you go. Keep in that format as long as possible.
- If, like me, you do copy editing on a Kindle or other eReader, it is simple to swap to a different style set on a copy of your manuscript (see later tip) and then create the eBook for your own purpose.

When you get to finalize your Smashwords doc, take these additional steps:

- First, remove all section breaks. Use the find and replace dialog (see screenshot below). Use the 'Special' button to Find 'Section Break' and replace with 'Manual Page Break. It really is as simple as that. *[Note that this only works one way. You cannot automatically find page breaks and replace with section breaks.]*
- Remove all headers and footers. Do this *after* removing all the sections. Make sure you remove all the headers and all the footers. Don't be caught out by that different first page footer you'd forgotten about. If you leave behind any headers or footers, you won't get into the Smashwords Premium Catalog.

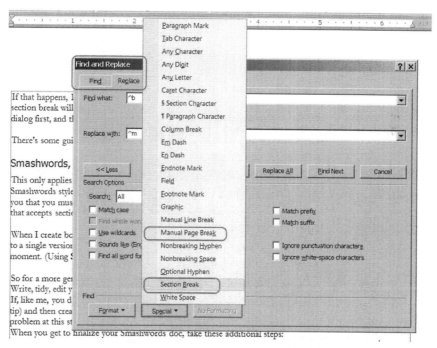

Figure 17: Use Find & Replace to quickly change break types

PAGE NUMBERS

We've talked a lot about headers and footers, but there are a few specifics to do with page numbers. Word 2007 introduced a new way to add page numbers and a new way to format them. They are a big improvement.

Users of earlier versions of Word have to approach page numbers differently, so I'll show how older versions do it too.

For Word 2007+ users, the simplest way is to open up the header/footer design menu on the Ribbon (by clicking on the header or footer area of the page) and clicking on the **Page Number** button as in this screenshot.

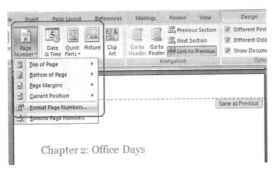

Figure 18: Word 2007/10/13 Page Number Button

Selecting the **Top of Page** or **Bottom of Page** options will give you a variety of pre-formatted page number field options in the header or footer respectively. Now, when I write *page number field*, what you are doing here is inserting a special *field code* that shows the number of the current page. In other words, when you view or print a page, Word works out which page you're on and substitutes that page number for the field code.

As for the other options: **Page Margins** offers fancy stuff, not recommended for straight fiction; **Current Position** puts a page number field where you currently have the cursor. You need to use this if your page number needs to share its header/footer with something else. For example, if you want book name and page number to both be on the header, you need to do something like this...

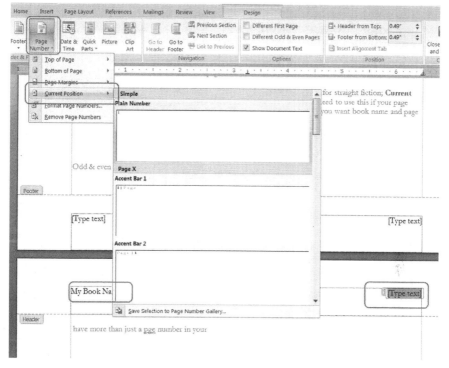

Figure 19: Word 2007/10/13 page number at current position

- In this example I've created a new header using the 'Blank (three columns)' option we saw in an earlier tip. On the left placeholder (where it says [Type Text]) I've put the book name.
- I selected the right-hand placeholder.
- I then select **Page Number** | **Current Position** This inserts a page number field into the right-hand placeholder.

The reason I've given this example is that if, instead, I had set up the three column header and then added page numbers using **Page Number** | **Top of Page**, Word would have deleted the rest of the header and left me with just the page number.

Make sure you have entered page numbers for ALL your headers/footers

It's easy to forget this. Say your header has different first page, odd page, and even page; now you want to add the footer and make it the same for all pages (except the blank ones). As far as Word is concerned, you *still have three different footers* (first page, odd, and even) and you need to define each one separately.

One gotcha that surfaced in my example novel of Andrew Cyrus Hudson's *Drift*, is that the opening chapters were short. So short that there weren't enough pages to show an even numbered page. I find the best approach is to add blank pages — just so I have enough to define all three headers and footers — and then delete the extra pages.

Formatting page numbers

On the Page Number Ribbon button we've just been looking at, one of the options is **Format Page Numbers...** which brings up the following dialog.

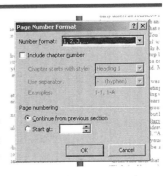

Figure 20: Format page numbers.

It does more than merely format the page number, as you can see. Go create a header or footer with a page number and play with this dialog until you're happy using it. It's quite obvious but I'll add a couple of tips:

- In this dialog you are setting options *for the current section*. As we saw earlier, the best approach is to set up your headers and footers, and other section options, for the section *at the start of the main body of your text*, and then use **link to previous** to copy your settings throughout the remainder of the book.

Front matter is all the stuff that goes before the main text of your book: copyright, title, half title, preface, introduction, acknowledgement, dedication, foreword... that sort of thing. [There's a section on front matter starting p196].

If you take a look at a variety of fiction and non-fiction books, you will see a range of strategies used to number the front matter pages. It's easy to allow yourself to get dismayed at the complexity of some book's front matter numbering, especially non-fiction reference books. Don't be! Let's take a moment to remind ourselves why we need page numbering at all.

The most important function of page numbers is to let you find the right page quickly. Take the book you're reading now. There are cross-references that take you to specific page numbers, a table of contents, and a table of figures. All these are very useful to find your way quickly around a reference book. In fact, I am certain they're useful because I use my own book as a reference when I'm working on book design, and I find the cross-references extremely useful.

If you've written a standard novel, then there is little value in tables of contents and cross-references because you expect your reader to start at the beginning of the book and keep reading until the end. Page numbers are much less important, but there are still a few reasons why they're useful:

- Readers can use page numbers to gauge the size of the book or the chapter, and to help estimate how long it will take to finish the current chapter.
- Readers can use page numbers to discuss a book with other readers or the author. For example, you could talk to me about 'the bit in your book about page numbers', but if you say 'on page 47, you said that...' then this makes communication much easier.

However, let's be honest. Although you should always have page numbers in standard novels because the book will look odd without them (and may be rejected by retailers) most readers will never use them. Bear that in mind as we go on to deal with page numbering with front matter. If you are publishing a conventional novel, most people will never read the page numbers.

Here, then are three common font-matter numbering approaches:

1. *This is the simplest approach. Use this unless you have a good reason to do otherwise.* Count the first page of the book as page 1, but don't display page numbers in the header or footer of the front matter. Instead you start displaying page numbers on the first page of the *main* section of your book. Page numbers should be shown as Arabic numerals ('1', '2', '3' etc). For example, if your book has Parts, and the page that says 'Part One' is the eighth page, then that's the first page that displays a page number in the footer. The page number to display is '8'. You don't display the page number for the first seven pages. Simple!

2. Take the same approach as with strategy#1 except when you start displaying page numbers, you always start with page '1'. In our example from strategy #1, we would start displaying page numbers on page 8 (as before) but this time, the footer at the bottom of the page that says 'Part One' would show '1' and not '8'. Some people think this is a

neater and possibly more honest approach. After all, the copyright page is not a part of the actual story, so why should that page be numbered as if it were? Some people think this way and some don't. I've given you this example so you don't think it's wrong if that's how you want to do it. However, it's simpler when the eighth page of your manuscript says 'page 8' at the bottom. There's no benefit in over-complication, so I would recommend strategy #1 over strategy#2.

3.   With this strategy, we start counting pages from the very first page, but we label the front matter pages with lower case Roman numerals ('i', 'ii' etc.) taking care not to display a page number for the half title (the very first page). When we get to the first page after the front matter, we restart the counting at '1' and start using Arabic numerals. This approach can make sense with non-fiction books where there are many pages of front matter. This is especially valuable when you have several sections of reference material in the front matter and you need page numbers so you can refer to them in the table of contents. Most books don't need this strategy, and using it without reason can make your book look over-fussy or pretentious. Reserve this approach for books that really need it.

Working with page numbers in Word 2003

Until Word 2007, you had to deal directly with the concept of *fields*. In fact, Word 2007/10/13 use fields in exactly the same way; it's just that the approach I've just described does all the hard work for you so you don't need to know what a field is.

With the earlier versions you need to place the cursor at the place where you want the page number in the header or footer, and then select from the main menu **Insert | Field**. (You can also bring up this dialog using **ALT + I, F**).

You will see a list of fields you can insert at this point (see screenshot below).

•   Scroll down and pick the field name, '**Page**'.
•   Click on the **Field Codes** button, and enter 'MERGEFORMAT', as I've done in the example screenshot below. The 'MERGEFORMAT' option tells Word to start counting its page numbers where it left off at the end of the previous section. If you don't, Word will start numbering each section at page#1.

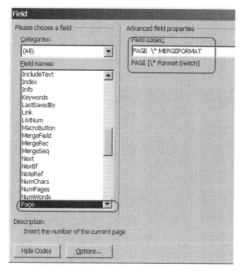

Figure 21: Adding the page fieldcode in Word 2003

If you're using Word 2007 or later, Word will do this 'mergeformat' malarkey for you automatically.

Of course, there may be places where you *want* Word to start numbering from page 1, most likely as you move from front matter to the main part of your book. In this case, you can change the field code option by clicking on the page number in your header or footer, and then **Right-click | Edit Field.**

For Word 2007+ users, this is all so much easier. You can set the starting page number for the current section with the **Page Number Format** dialog we saw earlier in this tip.

INTRODUCING STYLES

Styles are a means to define a set of formatting instructions, which you can then apply to parts of the document that you select. Suppose you decide you want your chapter headings to be Arial, 14 point, bold, small caps, spaced 12 points above, 6 below, and centered. You don't *have* to use styles at all. You could simply select each chapter heading paragraph, and repeat the set of formatting instructions.

What, though, if you have ninety chapters? Do you really want to repeat those instructions ninety times? Are you sure you could do that without making a mistake? Picture yourself banging your head against the fridge door because you've just gotten your proof copy in the mail and realize you forgot to apply small caps to chapter sixty-one.

Here's what I would do. Create a style — perhaps call it 'ChapterHeading' or maybe 'Heading 2' — and define the style as Arial, 14 point, bold, and all the other things we said earlier. Instead of applying the formatting to each chapter heading directly, apply the style instead. All the formatting comes with it for free.

And here's the real kicker... Perhaps when you get to upload your manuscript to Createspace, there's a problem embedding the font, or you realize you need a larger paragraph spacing for the chapter headings of the hardback edition, or you decide the font size should be larger... or any one of dozens of formatting instructions you want to change. With styles you change the style *definition* once; instantly, your change is applied to every paragraph set to follow that style. Without styles you have to find every location and change that paragraph individually; *and* you have to get it right every time. Using styles isn't just about saving you time: it's about producing books that are formatted *consistently*. And in this context, *consistent* and *professional* are synonyms.

Don't start from here! Start formatting as you write your book

You can save yourself a lot of grief later by picking the styles you will use and applying them as you write. If you don't use styles in your writing then now's the time to start. Also dividing the book into sections as you go, and setting headers and footers will save a little time too. By the way, this is even more true for eBooks, which have a habit of revealing subtly inconsistent formatting that is difficult or impossible to spot in Word or in paperback.

Don't worry about locking yourself down to a particular font or size, because you can easily modify the style definition at a later stage. Concentrate on becoming familiar with a set of styles, and apply them as you go. Microsoft Word has the Style Set concept, which is perfect for this. [See p137].

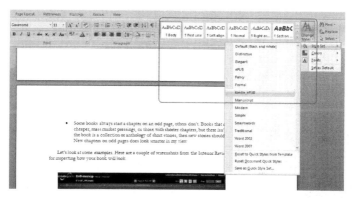

Figure 22: Styles and style sets in Word 2007/10

Figure 23 Styles sets have been promoted to their own gallery in Word 2013

The most important thing to know about **styles** is that it is worth investing your time to learn how to use them well.

It's a little like keeping your paperwork tidy and up to date as the year progresses, so that filing your tax return is no big deal. If you don't, and your records are scattered, lost, or plain wrong, then not only will you take far longer to do your tax return, but it will be more painful, and — crucially — you are far more likely to make mistakes.

Don't risk making mistakes with your printed book. Do yourself a favor and learn to use styles properly. After all, as I'm sure you'll agree, the biggest difference between your book layout and your tax return is that your book is far more important.

And if you're formatting eBooks as well as printed ones, that's doubly true.

In the remainder of Part 4, I'm going to be covering styles in the following sequence. In between, I'll cover other topics such as paragraph indentation and leading. That might appear a little random, but I've chosen that approach because it is precisely this type of paragraph formatting that you will want to implement with styles.

1. **Defining styles** — the mechanics of the thing in Microsoft Word.

2. **An example set of styles** you might use in printed books and eBooks.

3. **Using Style Sets** — Word 2007 and later only, I'm afraid. If you format a lot of books, especially if you move between Kindle, Smashwords, ePub, and print formats, Style Sets make life considerably easier and safer.

Defining Styles

Don't worry, I *am* going to explain how to define styles. But whatever I write here will become out of date, because every time Microsoft releases a new version of Word, they fiddle with the user experience for styles (because Microsoft realizes how vital styles are). And if you're using InDesign or Open Office then the concept of styles remains the same, but the implementation will be slightly different.

In other words, read these sections I'm giving you about styles, and then look at the detailed guidance in the help for your product.

Let's take a look around Word 2007 styles with a screenshot (By the way, Word 2010 and Word 2013 work exactly the same way. But when we get to stylesheets in a little while, I will show you how Word 2013 works differently).

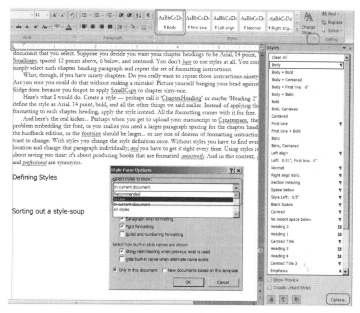

Figure 24: Styles in Word 2007/ 10/ 13

What I've done here is click on the little arrow at the bottom-right of the Styles area of the Ribbon. This launches the Styles Pane (which you see on the right, listing styles). I've then clicked on **Options...** at bottom-right of the Styles window, which has brought up the dialog box called **Style Pane Options**.

By default, **Select styles to show** (which tells Word what to show in the **Styles Pane** on the right) gives you *every style defined in the current document*. Most of the time, that's not what you want. So in the screenshot I'm about to change that to all styles **In use** in the current document.

I'm going to pause before going further. I've just blasted through a whole list of dialogs, windows, buttons, and options. If you aren't comfortable with styles then, yes, this will take a little while to get the hang of. Read my tips, but if you feel you only sort-of understand after the first read, open up your online help and browse through the topics I'm covering. Then have a play with a real (backed-up) Word document. It doesn't matter if it takes a few goes to get the hang of styles. The time you're investing will pay you back well.

So, back to our example we're running through. As you can see, I'm examining styles for the document you're reading. In the Style Pane Options dialog I chose to select styles to show **in use**, and I also de-selected **Font formatting** to leave only **Paragraph level formatting**. Once I've made these changes, the Styles Pane looks like this...

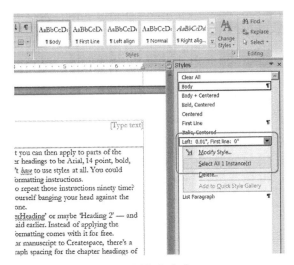

Figure 25: The Styles Pane

My Styles Pane now looks a lot less messy, and that's where you need to be. I would feel happier if all the styles in the Styles Pane were ones I created and I knew I was using. Right now I'm bothered by the one that labeled: *Left: 0.01", First Line: 0"*. When you see a style with a name like that, you can be sure it is direct formatting and not formatting from a style. Here I've clicked on the little button on the right of the style name in the Styles Pane and selected: 'Select All *n* Instance(s)'.

This shows me where this style is appearing. In this case, as with almost every example, this strange formatting is a mistake. So what I did next was to change the style to Body (by clicking on Body in the Styles Pane), which gets rid of this *Left: 0.01", First Line: 0"* forever.

Second Edition comment: why use styles again?

Several readers of the first edition of this book questioned the need to use styles at all. It's a fair question because if you were to eliminate all the direct formatting (such as the 'Left 0.01' example above) that could easily take over an hour if you have a lot of messy direct formatting to get through.

Here are two ideas to consider that I didn't mention in the first edition:

Firstly, if you have raggedy margins and occasional change of font, then this sort of thing can show up much more obviously in a paperback than when you're viewing your Word file on your computer monitor. If you don't tidy your styles, make sure to order a proof copy and have one inspection pass where you ignore the words you've written and look only at the formatting for every page. If you (and preferable a friend or two) can't see anything wrong, then you're good to go with the paperback version without needing styles.

But eBooks are a different matter altogether. The importance of tidy styles depends on how you are going to produce your eBook edition. If you or your eBook designer are going to strip the text down to html and then build up the styles through CSS classes, then consistent Word styles make no difference. If, however, you are going to upload your Word document to Amazon KDP, or run an automated conversion tool such as Calibre, Createspace, or Smashwords, then consistent styles can be crucial. Two paragraphs that might look identical on your monitor can come out very differently in the eBook. This is extremely confusing, but the reason is usually revealed when you look into the way the paragraphs have been styled. For example the gap between a heading and the body text below might be set by adding blank lines in one part of your book and by paragraph styling in another (using 'space below'). The two approaches could look indistinguishable in the paperback but wildly different in the eBook. Of course, you can always have a go without using consistent styles and carefully inspect the resulting eBook. But if you do this, work with the assumption that unless proven otherwise, any auto-formatted eBook is going to look bad unless you have styled Word consistently beforehand.

Defining Styles#1 — direct formatting into styles

If you've already started formatting your document, you can use it to generate styles automatically. You select a paragraph of text with formatting you want to reuse, and define a new style that will automatically copy across the formatting from your selected paragraph.

In the screenshot below, I've selected a paragraph (make sure you select the entire line) and then

Right-click | Styles... | Save Selection as a New Quick Style...

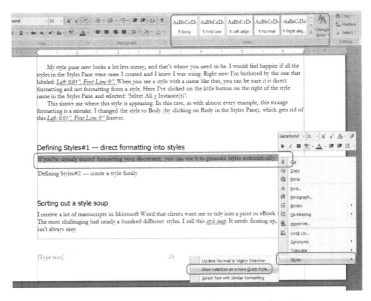

Figure 26: Creating a style from a selection in Word 2007/10

Quick Styles, by the way, are the style buttons on the Ribbon that I've ringed in the screenshot.

With Word 2013 you can do the same thing, but the screen works slightly differently. Select the paragraph and then **Right-click | Styles | Create a Style**

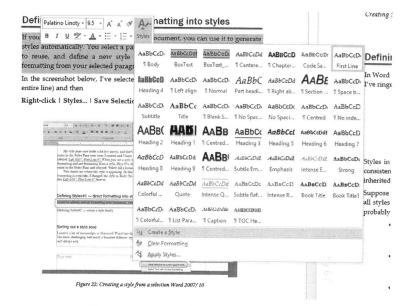

Figure 27: Creating a style from a selection in Word 2013.

In Word 2013, the term 'Style Gallery' replaced 'Quick Style' but means the same thing.

You can do something similar with Word 2003, but you'll need to look up *Creating Styles* in the online help. In fact, here's an online course to help you[4].

Defining Styles#2 — create a style family

In Word 2007-13, click on the button on the bottom-left of the **Styles Pane**, which I've ringed for you in this image.

---

[4] http://office.microsoft.com/en-us/word-help/format-your-document-with-styles-RZ001103924.aspx

Figure 28: Creating a new style

Styles in Word can *inherit* from other styles. That can be a great idea to aid consistency because if you make a change to a parent style, the characteristics inherited by its children change too.

Suppose I was starting to create my styles from scratch. Assume I have deleted all styles in the document except *Normal,* which is a special built-in style. I'd probably do something like this:

- Set my *Normal* style to a good, basic font. Let's say Garamond, 11pt, with a line spacing set to *At Least 12 pt* (see the section later on *Leading*).

- Create a new style — *Body* — that's based on *Normal* but has a first-line indent of 0.4". This means that Body will inherit the choice of Garamond, 11 pt from its parent.

- Create a new style — *First Para* — that's based on *Body* but has no first-line indent (used for first paragraph of scenes).

- Then I'd do something similar for headings and titles

- Create a style called *Title*. Arial, Bold, 18 pt, space above 24pt, space below 8 pt, Small Caps

- Create *Centered Title*, based on *Title* but centered.

- Create *Centered Title2*, based on *Centered Title* but take off the bold and lower font size to 16pt

- And so on... By the time you've figured out your title page, and the title page for each part, and your chapter headings, and the 'About the Author' bit at the end... you will find there are plenty of 'heading-type' fonts to define.

Why styles again?

Let's remind ourselves why we're putting this work in to define fonts...

Consider the heading styles in our example:

1. **Consistency.** We've defined headings to be Small Caps. If you did this manually, would you remember to set Small Caps every time? With styles, you don't have to remember or check: it will always follow the Small Caps rule.

2. **Changes are faster and safer.** Suppose you get all the way to uploading your finished manuscript to Createspace, only to find out that Createspace is complaining about your embedded fonts. What do you do? The safest thing is to use a different font, one that is embedded to Createspace's satisfaction. With styles, you only have to make this change once — to the *Title* style. All the heading styles we defined in our example are based on (inherit from) that *Title* style. So if we change *Title* from Arial font to, say, Belfast SF, then all our other title and heading styles also change to Belfast SF. That's powerful.

3. **Easily change between print, Kindle, and Smashwords editions.** I expect many of you also publish to Kindle and other eBook formats; each format has its own requirements and constraints. For example, Smashwords Premium Catalog format requires all fonts to be a maximum of 16 point, and often decides that if you vary the fonts throughout your document then it must be an error. With print format, you will probably want larger and fancier fonts for your chapter headings (compared with Smashwords) as well as much larger spacing from the top of the page down to your chapter heading. Print format will look very different, but if you have formatted your manuscript with styles, you can change most or all of your formatting between these various editions simply by redefining your styles.

4. **Lets you use style sets.** You need Word 2007 or later to use the supremely useful *style sets*. I've just explained how you can do most of your reformatting between print and Kindle editions by changing your style definitions. With style sets, you can change all your styles with just two clicks. (See p137)

Editing your styles

To change a style definition, right-click on the style name in the Styles section of the Ribbon, or on the style name in the **Style Pane** (the tall, narrow, window — usually on the right — with the title 'Styles')

Sorting out a style soup

I receive a lot of manuscripts in Microsoft Word that clients want me to tidy into a print or eBook format. The most challenging had nearly a hundred different styles. I call this *style soup*. It needs firming up, and that isn't always easy.

In the first case you need to go back to the **Style Pane Options** dialog and select the option to show **font formatting**. Remember when I took this option out in the earlier example in this section? Well, that was just to make the screenshots easier to read. You need to see all the fonts in use and thin them out until you're only left with those you are certain you need. Yes, that may take a while. It's best to do this as you write your book, not at the end.

In the great majority of cases, what you're doing here is taking some unwanted direct formatting and replacing with a defined style. Many experienced book formatters would argue that you should end up with a list only containing the styles that you defined. If you discover formatting you need, but isn't a straight style, then define a new style to cover this formatting. I've done this myself by adding formatting for italic and italic, right-aligned variants of standard styles.

Sorting out style soup... without losing your italics

Italics are the trickiest.

You can spot italics easily enough in the manuscript, but those slanted characters could have come about from a surprising number of sources. Here are a couple of tips for dealing with italics when tidying up a manuscript with a style soup:

- **Watch out for italic fonts** — *This problem is Windows-specific.* Most general-purpose fonts have a normally weighted typeface but have options for italic and bold weightings. It looks as if italics and bolds etc are all part of the same font, but that's Windows trying to simplify life for you. The hidden truth is that italics and bolds are defined in their own *separate* font files. With standard Windows and Office fonts this simplification works fine. But occasionally when you install fonts from elsewhere, the linkings are missing that would otherwise tell Windows how the italic, bold, and regular fonts are all part of the same typeface. You can get similar problems if opening a Word document in Windows that was originally written on a Mac. The end result is the same: characters could be italic because they are set in an italic-only typeface. Windows does not understand that they are italics and so the Find and Replace window will not detect them. This can confuse the next tip of counting italics.

- **Count your italics** — when applying style formatting to documents that were formatted without styles, the most likely problem you will encounter is accidentally losing your italics. Best thing you can do is count the number of italicized words before you apply styles, and then count them after to check the number matches. You'll soon know if you've lost some italics; backtrack until you find them and re-apply the italics. It's easy to do the counting. You need the **Find and Replace** dialog (CTRL + F).

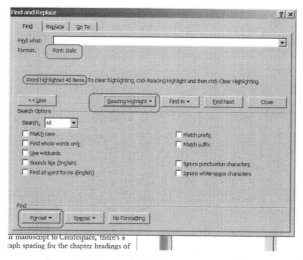

Figure 29: Using Find & Replace to count your italics

The steps I followed in this screenshot example are:

- Click on the **Format** button at bottom-left. Select **Font...** and then italic under **font styles**.

- Make sure the **Find what:** at the top is blank (because we want to search for formatting, not formatting + text)

- Click on the **Reading Highlight** button and **Highlight All**.

- Note down the count of hits you get back. In this case it was 40.

- Last of all, click on the **No Formatting** button at the bottom. Otherwise, the next time you try to Find something, Find and Replace will only return italic text.

JUSTIFICATION

I'm going to take a short break out of talking about styles to tell you some things you need to know in order to decide your style choices, starting with *justification*.

Justification is a typesetting alchemy that fits words within a column such that the words line up neatly against the left and against the right.

In fact, I'm going to give you a screenshot of the Wikipedia entry, (just look at the layout; you don't need to read the text) rather than format the paragraphs of the book you are reading, because if you are reading this in an eBook edition, *I cannot control how this book will be justified.*

Figure 30: The justified text is on the left.

The example on the left of the screenshot, *justified*, is what you want for print books. With Word, set the paragraph alignment to 'justified' (see screenshot below) and leave it at that. Remember to set the justification in your style definitions, not as direct formatting.

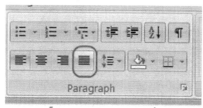

Figure 31: The 'justify' button.

Don't mess around with *optional breaking hyphens* and the like. If you know how to use them, you won't be reading this; if you don't know how to use them, leave well alone.

See the discussion about Adobe InDesign later in this book [p254] for a more detailed look at justification and hyphenation, because InDesign can deliver both at a more sophisticated level than Word.

Justification and eBook formatting

There are many badly formatted eBooks out there right now. I know; I've bought some. One of the worst offences is to get completely fouled up over justification, resulting in bogus hyphens everywhere and words split for no apparent reason. In short, an unreadable mess. This is caused by publishers setting up justification in their word processors or desktop publishing applications, and then the eReader device (such as a Kindle) trying to add its own justification.

The solution is simple: *if you are formatting an eBook edition of a manuscript,* ***don't justify the Word document.***

You should realize by now that this is simple to effect. For your eBook, set the style definitions to left-aligned. For the curious, this doesn't actually do what you probably think. Because left-aligned is the *default* alignment for Word (in most circumstances), the formatting information actually stored in your Word document actually says *unspecified* with regards to alignment. This is exactly what you are supposed to do according to Amazon's Kindle file formatting specification. What actually appears on the Kindle device (other devices are generally the same) is justified anyway. It's just that the justification has been set by the Kindle, and not by you.

The other thing to consider with eBook formatting is: *avoid very long words*.

A common example of very long words are when you spell out a URL; you know, a web address such as

http://www.amazon.com/Drift-Andrew-Cyrus-Hudson/dp/1468077899/ref=sr_1_1?ie=UTF8&qid=1328636231&sr=8-1

Most eBook readers will attempt to justify the text, but will be defeated by lines that contain a medium-sized URL. The example I've given is not long by any means, but is too long to fit in one line of the printed page. Now imagine you are reading this on an iPhone; every option for displaying that URL is going to look ugly.

You have four options to play with.

1. **Don't print out URLs.** For print books, put URLs in an appendix or keep them on your website. For eBooks, you are far better off embedding the hyperlink into shorter and more meaningful text such as *Drift*.

2. **Reduce the URL.** Many URLs have clutter on the end that you don't want. For example, to find *Drift* on Amazon.com, you can use this de-cluttered version: http://www.amazon.com/Drift-Andrew-Cyrus-Hudson/dp/1468077899 which points to exactly the same webpage.

3. **Place the URL on a separate line.**

4. **Reduce the font size.** Create a style called hyperlink (you may already have one) and make it a smaller font size.

PARAGRAPH INDENTATION

In fiction, there is a standard way to indent paragraphs. Don't take my word for it; go back to your bookshelf and check your own printed fiction books. What you will find looks like this:

Chapter 3: The Wedding

It was the tackiest restaurant they could have possibly picked. The building itself was probably made or redesigned in the 70's...early 80's? Either way, it must have been at least twenty-five or so years ago. The walls were that kind of wood paneling with the offbeat brown, stucco white ceilings aged in yellow, and wooden floors with some burgundy carpeting. But in a strange way, despite its poor taste, it had its own charm to it. At least the lighting wasn't so bad. Or maybe it was just because right here, right now, none of it really mattered.

"Congratulations, man."

The groom and the bride stood up to shake hands with Bryan Salesman and the date he brought along with him. There was no resting for the two of them, was there? Everyone had come from out of the woodworks to attend the wedding, each giving them their salutations.

"I didn't believe you when you said it, Travis. But hey, you did it. That makes you the first one out of all of us, doesn't it?"

"I don't know, has Simon tied the knot yet?"

"Why don't you ask him yourself?"

Bryan pointed behind him to Simon, who was waiting around to get a few words with the newlyweds.

"Well, well, well. It's been a long time, Travis, hasn't it?" Simon said. He was still cool, laidback, with an unwavering calm. A few hairs thinner and age creeping up too much for a man in his early thirties, but Simon was still Simon.

"I guess it has, hasn't it? How is the gaming industry?"

"Better than ever. How's the music business treating you? Any platinum albums yet?"

"Not yet, just starting out on producing. Still trying to decide on where to live."

"Well, that's always an important factor," Simon said. He then turned to the bride, shaking her hand. "And you must be the girl Travis has been talking about forever. Eileen, right?"

"The one and only. I'm Eileen," she said politely. "*Benson.*"

"And I'm Simon. *Florence.*"

They all laughed.

Figure 32: An example of paragraph indentation from 'Drift'.

- The first paragraph of a chapter *is not indented.*
- All following paragraphs *have their first line indented.*

- There are *no gaps between paragraphs.*

For printed fiction other than poetry, *you should treat this as a firm rule.* If, for example, you send the printed edition of your novel to a reviewer, and the first paragraph of your first chapter is first-line indented, then an LED will light up inside the reviewer's head. Underneath that LED will be the word: 'amateur'. Get it right!

Exceptions - other types of books

The 'other' way to format paragraphs is to not indent any of them, instead leaving a gap between paragraphs. However, while this is a fairly common way to format small documents in an office environment, this is not common with print books. I've just checked about twenty non-fiction print books and found only one that doesn't indent first lines. This was *Back Pain Remedies for Dummies*.

I expect you've seen the 'for Dummies' series yourself. It's a very popular series.

Why is paragraph spacing different for *Dummies*? The answer is that in writing — whether formatting or sentence construction — *clarity* is the ultimate goal that should drive your choices. The *Dummies* series has a lot of very short sections, inline images, and bullet point lists. They also use plenty of icons on the left-hand margin. It's far more broken up than a simple series of paragraphs such as you would find in a fiction book. And that is why *Dummies* books — and some other reference and text books — are not first-line indented.

At this point I expect you're itching to point out to me that the very book you are now reading follows this spacing-between-paragraphs approach. It does, and I decided on that approach because my words are broken down into nuggets of related thoughts, often presented as bullet points, and frequently broken by screen images. I expect readers to return to this book after a first read, looking to refresh their understanding of specific chunks of information. They will wish to zoom in on specific pieces of information, and this is helped by the visual cue of breaking clearly into thoughts (where one thought = one paragraph — mostly). It is similar, therefore, to a *Dummies* book, something with only short bursts of narrative discussion, and a book that will be treated as a reference work.

By contrast, the first edition of the eBook version was formatted differently, with first-line indents as with fiction. I chose that eBook approach because the reading area was much more limited in size with eReader devices, and I decided it was more important to the reader to fit more on the page.

Since the first edition, reading on tablets with larger screens than the old 600x800 pixel eReaders has become more common. And so I have changed the eBook paragraph spacing to also use the gap-between-paragraphs approach.

In other words, the layout of both editions has always been designed to maximize reading clarity.

Another type of book I have built for clients is the blog-to-book genre. Websites are often formatted with gaps between paragraphs and no first-line indent, and so it felt natural to use the same approach in the book version.

This paragraph indenting decision is the same as all aspects of writing: learn the rules; follow them by default, but be ready to break them if you are certain your way is better.

If you intend to follow this no first-line indent approach, be sure to read the topic about paragraph spacing [p 120].

Exceptions - scene breaks and letters

Let's assume you are following the standard for paragraph indentation. Well done, good choice.

Unfortunately, it is still not quite as simple as that. From time to time, you will encounter chapters broken down into scenes, and scenes broken down into smaller segments.

For scene breaks you need some white space (usually a single blank line) between paragraphs. Possibly you will add a centered asterisk [more on that on p183] but the question remains, do you indent the paragraph following the white space?

There again, what if your characters are reading from a letter? In the scene you shift repeatedly between narrative and dialogue, and the text of the letter. How should you indent the paragraphs of your letter? What about the first paragraph after your return from the letter to the narrative?

Having given you a firm rule earlier, I regret to inform you that there is no firm rule for this.

Actually there is. It's the default rule for all formatting, but it's still holds true:

- **Rule #1** Whatever is easiest to read is the best solution.

- **Rule #2** Having decided your approach, be consistent throughout the rest of your book, unless doing so contravenes rule one.

In case you're interested, here's what I do when formatting for my own Greyhart Press imprint.

- After a scene break, I do not first-line indent the first paragraph.
- After returning to the narrative following a letter, I do not first-line indent the first paragraph.
- I don't indent the first line of the first paragraph of letters, but do following paragraphs.
- I throw a blank line between narrative and letters.
- Of course, when I say 'letters' this could mean all sorts of weird things in the context of your book, anything you want to separate out from the main body of your narrative. Some examples: characters singing a song, a message coming over the radio, or memories being relived while the scene unfolds.

PARAGRAPH SPACING

You can use styles to specify a gap before and after each paragraph. Below, I've ringed the relevant sections of the Modify Style dialog. To bring this up you modify style (for example by selecting the menu in the **Styles Pane** on the right) and then **Format | Paragraph...**

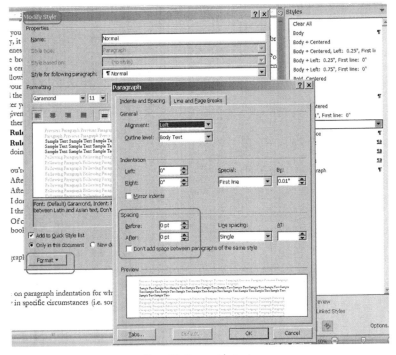

Figure 33: Paragraph spacing

For the most part, this really is as simple as it looks. Have a play if you've not used this before to see the results. You might be asking the question, why bother?

After all, if we like our chapter headings to appear some way down the page, we could simply type a few carriage returns (press the Return or Enter key a few times) for the same effect.

Well, you would be right that you would get the same result with the *printed* editions of your books. There are three very good reasons why you should take the trouble to define paragraph spacing in styles.

1. Consistency
2. Maintainability
3. eBook editions

Let's look at an example to make this feel real, and then come back to the three reasons in turn. We'll see Chapter 3 of *Drift* in Adobe Reader (a viewer for PDF files), and then we'll see the same page in Microsoft Word.

Chapter 3: The Wedding

It was the tackiest restaurant they could have possibly picked. The building itself was probably made or redesigned in the 70's…early 80's? Either way, it must have been at least twenty-five or so years ago. The walls were that kind of wood paneling with the offbeat brown, stucco white ceilings aged in yellow, and wooden floors with some burgundy carpeting. But in a strange way, despite its poor taste, it had its own charm to it. At least the lighting wasn't so bad. Or maybe it was just because right here, right now, none of it really mattered.

"Congratulations, man."

The groom and the bride stood up to shake hands with Bryan Salesman and the date he brought along with him. There was no resting for the two of them, was there? Everyone had come from out of the woodworks to attend the wedding, each giving them their salutations.

"I didn't believe you when you said it, Travis. But hey, you did it. That makes you the first one out of all of us, doesn't it?"

"I don't know, has Simon tied the knot yet?"

"Why don't you ask him yourself?"

Bryan pointed behind him to Simon, who was waiting around to get a few words with the newlyweds.

"Well, well, well. It's been a long time. Travis, hasn't it?" Simon said. He was still cool, laidback, with an unwavering calm. A few hairs thinner and age creeping up too much for a man in his early thirties, but Simon was still Simon.

"I guess it has, hasn't it? How is the gaming industry?"

"Better than ever. How's the music business treating you? Any platinum albums yet?"

"Not yet, just starting out on producing. Still trying to decide on where to live."

"Well, that's always an important factor," Simon said. He then turned to the bride, shaking her hand. "And you must be the girl Travis has been talking about forever. Eileen, right?"

"The one and only. I'm Eileen," she said politely. "*Benson*."

"And I'm Simon. *Florence*."

They all laughed.

Figure 34: Paragraphs — worked example in Adobe Reader

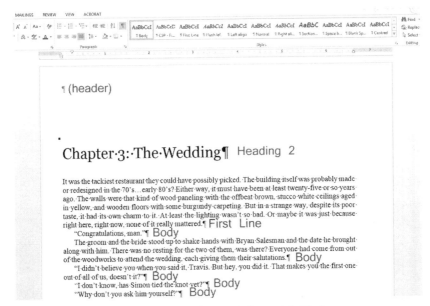

Figure 35: Paragraphs — worked example in Word

That symbol that looks like the mirror image of a filled-in 'P' (a 'Pilcrow') is a paragraph mark. It marks the end of a paragraph. There's a button on the Ribbon which has this paragraph symbol; clicking it shows up formatting information such as paragraphs. In fact, that's why I've clicked it here: so you can see how I've broken down the top of chapter 3 into paragraphs.

From the top of the page, my paragraphs are:

1. One paragraph in *Heading 2* style — Remember just now I showed you how to define paragraph spacing? I've defined *Heading 2* to be **Spacing Before**: 72pt and **Spacing After**: 24pt.

2. One paragraph of *First Line* style — This is a style I've created by inheriting from *Body* style but changing to have no indentation. I use this for the first paragraph of a chapter.

3. All the paragraphs after that are *Body* style.

Consistency, maintainability, eBooks: they were the reasons I gave for using styles rather than blank lines.

Consistency

Let's see the top of Chapter 3 without using paragraph spacing:

Figure 36: Paragraphs worked example — spacing for chapter headings.

Here I have five blank lines before the chapter title. You could do this throughout the book, but are you sure you've always added five blank lines? Are you sure you haven't sometimes used four or six?

Then look at the paragraph markers; one is larger. This is very common thing to get wrong. When I added the first blank line (by hitting the Enter key) Word decided at first that I wanted another paragraph of *Heading 2* style. That's why one of the paragraph markers is bigger: it's a bigger font... *it's a taller line*. It isn't enough to always have five blank lines, you also have to be certain that they are same style.

Hence *consistency*. If you used paragraph spacing as I did originally, your chapter headings are more likely to appear the same distance down the page.

Maintainability

Suppose you had happily produced a mass market paperback edition and didn't use paragraph styling. Now you want an 8" x 10" hardback. Your page size is now larger and you have a lot of choices to make regarding how you will format this new layout. You might decide to present your chapter headings farther down the page. Perhaps instead of six blank paragraphs before each chapter heading you now want eight. You have to do this for every chapter. If you use styles, all you need to change is the *Heading 2* style definition, altering the paragraph spacing until you are happy.

eBooks

Suppose you make a Kindle edition of your book. That Kindle-format book might be read on an iPhone, iPad, Kindle, and Mac or other device, and each user will select different display options. With eBooks you cannot make assumptions about the page size. It could be very small, and that means you can't have big gaps before Chapter headings (for example) because that will look terrible on some devices. What's more, putting several blank lines together in sequence is forbidden by the Smashwords Premium Catalog rules — your eBook will be rejected.

So if you want an eBook and a print version of your book, controlling the spacing through styles makes it much easier to convert one format to another.

And there's more. With many popular routes of getting from Word into eBook format, the blank lines you see in your Word or printed book *are stripped out*. In case you were wondering, if you inserting manual line breaks (Windows: Shift + Enter; Mac: Shift + Return), they get stripped out too.

If you want to have blank space before chapter headers and between scenes, there is only one reliable way to do this, and that is by using paragraph spacing. And the way to implement paragraph spacing consistently and with easy maintenance is to do so using styles.

The paragraph spacing gotcha

A little earlier, I showed you Chapter 3 of *Drift* broken down into paragraphs. I've set the chapter heading down the page somewhat by entering a value into the space above property of the Heading2 style.

That all looks fine, but sometimes you look at a page and realize that your Heading2 paragraph is right at the top of the page. You check the paragraph setting and, yes, there really is a 72pt space before the paragraph. Where has it gone?

There is a peculiar feature in Word that sometimes means it does not respect the paragraph spacing before the paragraph that you defined in your style.

If the preceding paragraph has spacing *after*, then any paragraph spacing *before* in the current paragraph is ignored. I don't blame you if you want to read that sentence again! Ouch!

A simple way to address this is to have a blank line of a style (such as *Normal*) that has no paragraph spacing.

Prior to Word 2013, there used to be an alternate solution that involved adding a page break before my chapter heading, and going into Word Options to turn off the option to suppress spacing at top of page. I've suggested doing this in the past, but in Word 2013, that is no longer a reliable solution.

So what I tend to do myself with Word 2013 is use *section breaks* before a heading that I know will be the first paragraph on the page, and needs spacing before. This requires you to be comfortable with sections, but will always work.

Microsoft Word and 'The Black Spot' ...

If you turn on the show/hide option, you will probably see some mysterious small black squares in the left margin. In our screenshots in this section that 'black spot' is to the left of the paragraph that reads: 'Chapter 3'.

It might be mysterious, but isn't very interesting to most authors and you can safely ignore it.

Word adds that spot against any paragraph that is styled with one of these options:

- Keep Lines Together

- Keep With Next

- Page Break Before

- Suppress Line Numbers

Heading styles by default have 'keep with next' and so that's why you see the spot here.

A STARTING SET OF STYLES

These are the styles I use.

- **Body** — default font with addition of first-line indent and justified alignment. I have body-italic defined as a variant too, although that's mainly to help me build eBooks.
- **First Paragraph** — inherited from *Body* but with no first-line indent. Use this for the first paragraph of a chapter. I call this style *First Line*, which really isn't a good name but I'm used to it, and you will see that name in screenshots.
- **Centered** — inherited from *Body* but with centered alignment AND no first-line indent. I use this for images as well as centered text.
- **Headings** — I use *Heading 1, Heading 2,* and *Heading 3,* which are built-in styles I modify for my use. These styles have paragraph spacing before and after.
- **Blank Space** — inherited from *Centered* but with paragraph spacing defined as 6pt above and 6pt below. I use this to define blank lines and scene breaks with asterisks. I use *Blank Space* style rather than enter blank lines to achieve spacing because this is much safer if you ever want to produce an eBook edition directly from your Word file.

I use other styles too, but I don't wish to over-complicate so I've given what I regard as the essential set.

By the way, that list you've just read uses *List Paragraph* style. The gap after the list was *Blank Space*. You're reading a *Body* style paragraph right now. If this were fiction then the paragraph above would have been *First Line* (i.e. unindented) and this *Body* style paragraph would be first-line indented.

Other styles I use include bulleted lists, title styles for the front page, styles for headers and footers, reduced font-size styles for notes and front matter (such as copyright information, especially if you're laying out an anthology).

In fact, I make sure that every paragraph in books I format is defined by a style that I created, except for the main title and half title at the beginning of the book. If you are only formatting a print book, then that might be overkill because what you see on the screen in Word's print layout, or with your PDF export is going to be what comes out in the book. Not so if you're going to produce an eBook edition, where what comes out in the eBook could bear little resemblance to what you see in Word if you aren't careful.

I use the **Styles Pane** to check the styles that are actually in use. If I don't recognize them, I examine where they are used (the **Select All *n* Instance(s)** you see in the screenshot below). I most cases I replace with styles I defined myself. Make sure you've set the Styles Pane to show all styles in use for both paragraph and font level formatting (click on the **Manage Styles** button at the bottom of the Styles Pane to set this).

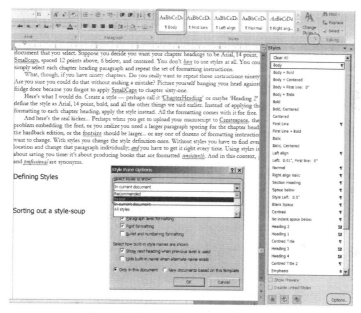

Figure 37: Filtering Style Pane to 'styles in use'.

FONTS AND TYPEFACES

In Part 7 of this book, I delve into the basics of typography (the art and science of fonts) in TYPOGRAPHY 101 [p213], and in some more detail in TYPOGRAPHY 909 [p225]. That's for later. Here I want to answer a question I'm often asked: which fonts should I use for my book?

I'm going to give you some suggestions, picking fonts that are free online (Open Source fonts) or provided by Microsoft through Microsoft Office (and in one case Microsoft Windows). Please use these suggestions as a starting point. Try variations of font and other design choices for yourself and get them printed in a private test project on Createspace because there is absolutely no substitute for eyeballing the finished design in print.

One common theme in the font suggestions is that the body text (the main text of your book) is set in a SERIF font. Serifs are the little lines on the end of character strokes. A font without serifs is called SANS-SERIF (or occasionally Gothic or Grotesque). Other than large-type children's books and poetry, you should choose a serif font for your body text. Large blocks of text (e.g. novels) are simply easier to read with a serif font. Centuries of experience has shown that to be the case and this is one thing that the digital age has not changed.

The best way to show the difference between serif and sans-serif is with an example. Here's the DejaVu set of fonts.

The DejaVu Family

DejaVu Serif

DejaVu Sans

DejaVu Mono

The third DejaVu font is a MONOSPACE or FIXED-WIDTH font, so called because each letter takes the same width on the page. That's how typewriters work, and indeed they are sometimes called 'typewriter fonts'. You should have a monospace font called Courier New, and that's a good option for separating out from the main body text in your book passages that are meant to be typewritten, or on a computer screen.

Monospace fonts such as Courier New and Prestige Elite can also work well for chapter titles, say for a hardboiled detective novel in the 1930s or a Cold War spy thriller. If you search online for (legal) free font downloads, you will find distressed typewriter fonts for just this purpose. The characters are worn away slightly as if the ink on the typewriter ribbon is running out.

Let's see some more examples:

CHAPTER 13

LOREM IPSUM. PROIN GRAVIDA nibh vel velit auctor aliquet. Aenean sollicitudin, lorem quis bibendum auctor, nisi elit consequat ipsum, nec sagittis sem nibh id elit. Duis sed odio sit amet nibh vulputate cursus a sit amet mauris. Morbi accumsan ipsum velit. Nam nec tellus a odio tincidunt auctor a ornare odio. Sed non mauris vitae erat consequat auctor eu in elit. Class aptent taciti sociosqu ad litora torquent per conubia nostra, per inceptos himenaeos. Mauris in erat justo. Nullam ac urna eu felis . . .

FONTIN *Fontin SmallCaps (title). Fontin (body text).*
Fontin sans (this note)

The first example uses Fontin, which is an open source set of fonts that don't come with Microsoft Office, but is freely available to download online from font sites such as www.fontsquirrel.com . Fontin is unusual in that it has a version of the font specifically for small caps. With most fonts, people usually use faux small caps, but that's a topic for Typography 101 on [p220]. I feel it has a heavy and slightly dark feel to it, which naturally suits some purposes and not others.

Chapter 13

LOREM IPSUM. PROIN GRAVIDA nibh vel velit auctor aliquet. Aenean sollicitudin, lorem quis bibendum auctor, nisi elit consequat ipsum, nec sagittis sem nibh id elit. Duis sed odio sit amet nibh vulputate cursus a sit amet mauris. Morbi accumsan ipsum velit. Nam nec tellus a odio tincidunt auctor a ornare odio. Sed non mauris vitae erat consequat auctor eu in elit. Class aptent taciti sociosqu ad litora torquent per conubia nostra, per inceptos himenaeos. Mauris in erat justo. Nullam ac urna eu felis . . .

Palatino/Eurostile: Eurostile(title). Palatino Linotype (body text - use 'Palatino' on Mac). Arial (this note).

In the second example I've used Palatino Linotype for the body text (if you don't have this font on the Mac, use 'Palatino' instead). Palatino Linotype is a great workhorse for books, suiting most purposes. It's the font I'm using for the print edition of the book you're reading now. I've paired it with Eurostile for the chapter heading, which gives strength and manages to be both retro and technological. This could be a good look for a techno-thriller, science fiction, and many types of non-fiction.

I've used Arial for the note at the bottom. It's sans serif while the main body is serif. But more than that, it's a very different design from Palatino Linotype, which makes it stand out as something separate. Compare with the previous example that used Fontin serif for the main text and Fontin sans serif for the note. You should see that the Arial note stands out more. Whether that is a good thing or not depends on what goal your typography choices are helping you to achieve.

Chapter 13

LOREM IPSUM. PROIN GRAVIDA nibh vel velit auctor aliquet. Aenean sollicitudin, lorem quis bibendum auctor, nisi elit consequat ipsum, nec sagittis sem nibh id elit. Duis sed odio sit amet nibh vulputate cursus a sit amet mauris. Morbi accumsan ipsum velit. Nam nec tellus a odio tincidunt auctor a ornare odio. Sed non mauris vitae erat consequat auctor eu in elit. Class aptent taciti sociosqu ad litora torquent per conubia nostra, per inceptos himenaeos. Mauris in erat justo. Nullam ac urna eu felis . . .

Garamond/Gabriola: Gabriola(title). Garamond (body text). Candara (this note).

For the final example, I've used Garamond, an excellent choice for body text, lighter than the other examples and can work well for titles too. For the chapter heading I've used Gabriola, a beautiful font from Microsoft that comes with Office 2010 and later (and Windows 7 and later). Gabriola is elegant and romantic but still easy to read for titles and short passages of text. This combination would work well for a romance or fantasy novel.

Where I list the fonts at the bottom, I've used Candara because it has a completely different feel to Gabriola and Garamond. That's a good technique for some non-fiction, to have notes, asides, and sub headings in a different font that stands out from the main body text. In the book you're reading now, I use Franklin Gothic Medium for the headings, Palatino Linotype for body text, but I switch to 'Calibri (Light)' for the notes in text boxes.

The Gabriola font contains 4,500 characters and makes use of many of the new OpenType features we'll see later in TYPOGRAPHY 101 [p213]. In particular, it uses seven different STYLISTIC SETS, each of which provides variations on the font design that become increasingly fancy.

In the line below, I've used some of these stylistic sets to achieve an elegant yet still highly readable look. For use in historical fiction perhaps?

One of the main differences between the Gabriola stylistic sets is the amount to which serifs and tails are exaggerated. Look at the 'y' and the 'l', but also in a more subtle way the 'D' and the 'b'. These exaggerated strokes are called SWASH. It is only with the 2010 edition that Word could first access OpenType features such as stylistic sets, and Microsoft has been reworking some old fonts (such as *Impact*) to make use of them. The flourishes to either side of the text are part of the Gabriola font too. To insert them I used INSERT | SYMBOL from the Ribbon. They aren't images, they are glyphs (characters) in a font. If you're reading the eBook edition, those flourishes won't appear properly. That's because they are symbols peculiar to the Gabriola font and that font does not exist on your reader. So that everyone can see what I'm talking about, here's a screenshot of the Gabriola text.

articular, it uses seven different stylistic sets, which are variations on th(
)nt design that become increasingly elegant.

1 the line below, I've used some of the stylistic sets to achieve an elegan
et still highly readable look. Historical fiction perhaps?

Figure 38: Gabriola font demonstrating swash and ornaments.

Later on [p 154] I will talk about using Unicode code points to produce symbols that look good in print and will also show up on most eBook readers and tablets. Those Gabriola flourishes are examples of glyphs that are not standard Unicode code points and so will definitely not show up in your eBook.

Where to find fonts

There are various places to find fonts to download. Adobe.com is a very popular choice for professionals. Good fonts aren't cheap, but Adobe is currently doing a couple of value font packs that get you very good quality fonts for around $55 for the set.

For free fonts, try www.FontSquirrel.com

For free font recommendations, try www.smashingmagazine.com . Although its emphasis is on web design, it does recommend free fonts suitable for books.

Is it worth paying for fonts when your computer comes with free fonts? It depends on personal taste. The fonts that come with Windows, Microsoft Office and MacOS are perfectly good quality for most uses. Some of the fonts you can download from the internet for free, or for a small donation are good too, but a few look rough, especially when used for titles. It is with titles, though, that we normally have a little more license to use more dramatic fonts. (By 'titles' that typically means the title page in your front matter, part titles and chapter titles).

In the past year I've become a fan of Adobe Garamond Pro and Adobe Text Pro, neither of which are free (although they might be bundled for free with other Adobe products you might have bought, such as Adobe Photoshop). I like the fact that they look good whatever size I set them to.

I know I'm repeating myself, but if you are unsure of font choices, try some out in a test project on Createspace and get a proof copy sent to you. If your choice of font or leading is poor, your gut instinct will tell you straight away (as will your friends and family).

LEADING

Leading is one of those strange typesetter's terms that you would probably call *line spacing*, or *line sizing*. The word comes from the days when line spacing was implemented by adding strips of lead between the lines of type (which is why it's pronounced 'ledding' and not 'leeding'). If you've ever submitted a manuscript to an editor or publisher, you've probably used *double spacing*. All that means is that the lines are twice as high as normal.

On the Word Ribbon is the Paragraph menu, where you set such things as alignment and bullets. You should see a little button with arrows pointing up and down; that's the line spacing button. Have a play with it now and see the effect it has on your paragraphs.

For your books, you want to set the line spacing to be slightly larger than the font size. In other words, you're adding *leading*. How much is a personal setting, but you probably want to do something because books with no leading and small-ish font sizes (and small margins, for that matter) are generally mass-market books trying to cut costs by reducing the page count. You can't compete on price with mass-market books, so it's worth being fairly generous with your leading to make your book look higher quality.

The correct way to apply leading, of course, is not through that little button; it is through styles.

If you **Modify...** styles as we've seen before, select **Format | Paragraph** to bring up the following...

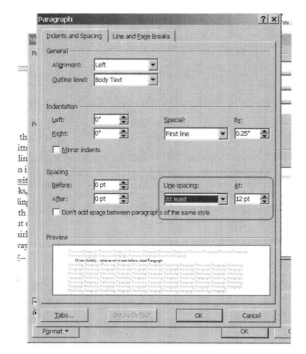

Figure 39: Setting line spacing (leading)

In my default Createspace Style Set, I have my body text set to 11pt. So what I do is modify the *Normal Style* and set the line spacing to *At least 12pt*, as in the screenshot about. The other styles *inherit from Normal*, and so they also have a line spacing set to at least 12pt. All this means, is that the height of the lines is set as if the font for the text in that line was always at least 12pt. It doesn't matter whether your text is 9pt, 10 or 11, the lines are as tall as if you had 12pt text.

If you have a heading with a larger font than 12pt, then the line height is not shrunk, because you have set the line spacing to be *At least* and not *Exactly* 12pt.

If you set body text to 11pt Garamond, then you might also try line spacing at 13 pt. Any more and it feels excessive to me. But it's your book! I also like Adobe Garamond Pro at 11.5pt and 13pt spacing (yes, you don't have to set your font size to whole numbers of points!). Experiment with a variety of fonts and font sizes. For a more traditional look, for example, try the slightly heavier Berling Antiqua at 12 point, with 14 point leading.

In most cases, you will want your line spacing to be set to *At least* slightly larger than your body text size.

Top tip for choosing your typeface, size, and leading

You can spend all day reading other people's favorite font recipes, but there is no substitute for seeing it for yourself. Viewing your pages on your computer monitor isn't good enough. You have to see how your fonts and leading looks in an actual book.

So here's what you do. (You've heard me say this before, and by this point in the book you know enough to go out and do it…)

Create a new project in Createspace. Call it 'Font Test' or some such. It doesn't matter what you call it because you will never make this book available to the public.

Add one chapter to your book using one of your possible typeface size/ leading options. Don't just do one page, do several.

Then repeat for multiple chapters, each one with a different font / leading option.

Order a proof copy and inspect the result to pick the layout option you prefer.

Keep the project for every time you want to try out a new font or new layout option. Keep the proof copy too for reference.

---

eBooks and leading

Warning! With eBooks. I would avoid leading altogether for body text as the results across various devices are unpredictable.

Specifically, Smashwords say they will reject your book from their Premium Catalog if you set the line spacing to anything other than Single, although one of the earlier readers of this book reports she sets line spacing to 1.5 times and has no problem with Smashwords.

What you really want is a way to preserve different sets of styles for different formatting tasks — and to be able to switch seamlessly between them… which bring us to our next topic, *Style Sets*.

SUPER STYLE SETS

Word 2007 introduced the idea of Style Sets. If you want several different layouts for the same book manuscript (for example, hardback, paperback, Kindle, ePub, and Smashwords) then style sets are a must-have. If you've not thought about them much, you're going to love this section.

Style sets and Word 2013

The screenshots below are from Word 2007. When I first loaded up Word 2013, my heart skipped a beat. Style sets weren't there! In fact, they are but have been moved from the HOME Ribbon menu to the new DESIGN menu. This is a promotion because style sets now have their own section of the Design menu where you can pick from a gallery of Microsoft-designed, and your customized style sets.

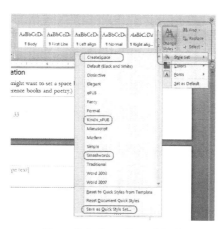

Figure 40: Style sets I have defined.

From the styles section of the Ribbon, click **Change Styles | Style Set** to bring up the window in the screenshot. The idea is that you pick a predefined set of styles from the list. Where a style is used in your document *and* it is defined in the new style set, the old formatting is replaced with the new definition.

For example, what you are reading right now is a paragraph that uses the style called *Body*. I've defined *Body* to use the font Garamond.

Now, there's a style set that came out of the box with Word 2007 called, appropriately, *Word 2007* (It's still available as a style set in Word 2010 and Word 2013). This Word 2007 style set also has a definition for a style called *Body*, except there the font is defined as Calibri. If I picked Word 2007 from the Style Set window you see in the screenshot above, then this paragraph would instantly switch from Garamond to Calibri. My headings too would switch to Cambria, and some would be colored blue (because the document would now follow the new definitions for *Heading 1*, *Heading 2* etc.)

If you're scratching your head at this point, simply take a copy of a document with styles you have defined, and start picking different style sets to see what happens.

Using style sets with your book

In my list of style sets, I have the following:

- **Createspace** — Titles and headings have fancier fonts, large font sizes, large paragraph spacing above. Fonts used are those I have successfully embedded into PDF and then uploaded to Createspace.
- **Kindle_ePub** — In comparison with the Createspace style set, fonts are smaller and simpler. Titles and headings have much smaller paragraph spacing.
- **Smashwords** — Very similar to Kindle_ePub except maximum font size set to 14 point, and less variation between font sizes (because if you use a variety of fonts, Smashwords sometimes decides that is a formatting error and rejects your book).

If I've created my print layout first, and now I want to start formatting for a Kindle edition, the first thing I do is change to the Kindle style set; all my style definitions are instantly changed to something appropriate for the Kindle.

There is also a *Manuscript* style set. It comes out the box, but I've altered it for standard manuscript format with Courier typeface and double line spacing. I use this to send my own manuscripts to editors and my agent.

To make all this magic work, you have to remember to use the same set of style names. Suppose I had defined a style called *ChapterHead,* and assigned that to all my chapter headings. I have to use exactly the same style name (ChapterHead) in my Createspace, Kindle_ePub, and Smashwords style sets. Otherwise, when you pick a new style set, your formatting won't change.

Creating your own style sets

You will see that Word has several style sets that come out the box. In the screenshot above, I've ringed a few that I've created. To create your own, first define your styles to your satisfaction, and then click **Save as Quick Style Set**.

To update an existing style set in 2007 & 2010, click **Save as Quick Style Set** and overwrite an existing style set.

These style set files will become valuable, so *back them up.*

To save a new style set in in Word 2013, go to the DESIGN menu on the Ribbon and click on the 'more' button at the bottom-right of the style set gallery (it looks like a downward-pointing triangle with a line on top).

To save, click on **Save as a New Style set...**

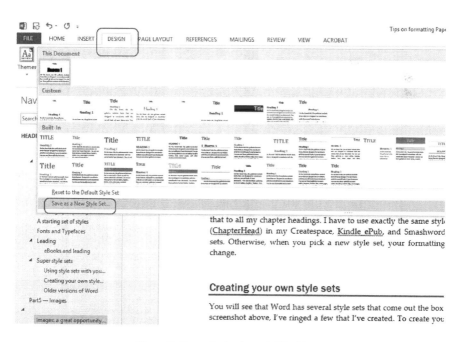

Figure 41: Customized style sets in Word 2013.

Older versions of Word

If you're using Word 2003 or earlier, you'll have to sit this one out. There was a concept of importing styles from global templates. If you're a Word geek, look it up[5] and try it out. Personally, I always found it too complicated to use. Style sets are much better. Upgrade.

---

[5] http://office.microsoft.com/en-us/word-help/previewing-templates-using-the-style-gallery-HA001146639.aspx

Part 5 — Images

A great opportunity but Word lets you down •
Where to use images • *Typographer's ornaments*
• *Color images & bleed* • *How to insert images* •
*How Microsoft Word ruins your images (if you're
running Windows)* • *Third-party PDF drivers* •
Working with images < 300dpi

Images with Word and Createspace

It is easy to insert images into your Word document, and Createspace will print them with no extra charge. Appropriate use of images can enhance the quality of your book.

If you require large, high quality images in your book, then you could have a problem because Microsoft strews obstacles in Word's way when you want to handle high quality images. This is a particularly bad problem if you're running Word on the Windows operating system. Read on to learn what this means and what you can do about it.

IMAGES: A GREAT OPPORTUNITY BUT WORD LETS YOU DOWN

You can use images to enhance the reading experience for your book. Let's be realistic, though, you can also misuse images to make your book look ridiculous.

I'll cover how you can insert images and wrap text around them. I'll explain how to set captions too, such as you'll see in the book you're reading now (if you're reading the paperback version). In fact, putting in the images is the easy part. What requires more thought is:

- Selecting appropriate uses for images for your book. There might be more opportunities than you realize.
- How to work around the limitations Microsoft has built into Word's handling of images, although this problem is less acute with some more recent editions of Word.

We'll cover each topic in turn, but since I've raised the issue of Word's limitations regarding images, I'll summarize the problem and solution here.

For large, crisp images in your paperback, you want images at a minimum resolution of 300dpi. However, if your only images are an author photo in your bio at the back, and cover images of your other books in the 'other books by...' section, then many authors find printing images at 200dpi gives acceptable results.

Versions of Microsoft Word prior to Word 2010 always downgrade your images to a maximum of 220dpi. There is no way around this.

Versions of Microsoft Word from 2010 onwards allow you to save images inside your document without downgrading the dpi resolution. You have to tell Word to do this.

On the Windows operating system, Microsoft Word versions 2007, 2010, and 2013 all allow export to the PDF file format, which is what I recommend to upload to Createspace. However, all of them, including 2013, downgrade the resolution of your images to 199dpi when they create the PDF. If you want the PDF to have images at 300dpi, then you need to either buy a third-party PDF printer driver or Adobe Acrobat. Alternatively find someone who can produce 300dpi PDFs — maybe a friend or colleague or a professional — to take your Word file and build the PDF for you. Or you can try uploading your Word document directly to Createspace without first creating a PDF.

On the Mac, since the 2007 release of OS X, Apple has provided a PDF export facility built into the operating system. Don't use Microsoft's PDF export, instead use Apple's 'save to PDF' printer driver option. And while you're at it, select PDF/x format too.

Why, oh why, does Microsoft limit Word in this way?

Actually, I've a shrewd idea. Microsoft has a product in their Office range called Microsoft Publisher. It's their desktop publishing software for high quality digital printing. Being able to create PDFs with images at resolutions of at least 300dpi is a core requirement for desktop publishing software.

I'd better stop there before I get sued. Actually, I do have more to say. Don't mistake me for indulging in the popular pastime of Microsoft bashing here. I think Microsoft Word is a fantastic product that gets better and better and Microsoft has pushed it deep into the territory that was once the preserve of desktop publishing software and typesetting tools such as Adobe InDesign. This isn't the only limitation of Word — I'll come to the others (faux small caps, hyphenation, vertical justification) as we go through the book — but the inability to natively produce 300dpi PDFs is the only one that could be a serious enough issue for some authors that they would need to buy third-party PDF software to fix it.

WHERE TO USE IMAGES

Outside of the front and back matter, most adult novels don't need images. In fact, I would go further and say most adult novels *should not* use images in the main body because they will look silly, an overdesigned book where the over-elaborate design distracts the reader from the text.

Other types of books benefit enormously from images. How-to guides can often be a very dry series of bullet points unless lifted up by illustration, icons, diagrams and pull quotes. I read a lot of children's fiction to my seven year old. Some of the design is brilliant and becomes such a vital element of the feel of the book that it's difficult to imagine how it would feel without the images. The *Scream Street* series by Tommy Donbavand with its dirty thumbprints, lurking spiders and distinctive style of illustration is a superb example of the design possibilities with images.

Of course, if you're writing an illustrated children's book, or a travel guide with a stack of photos, then you already know that images are critical to the story your book is telling.

In this section I'll run through some examples of where to use images. Perhaps you will find an idea that hasn't occurred to you.

Once you've read this section, take a look at the books on your bookshelf and take a visit to the library. Look for how your competitors' books use images.

Images: break free of convention

"Deeply, deeply conservative."

That's how typesetters who lay out print books for major publishers are sometimes perceived by other people learning the basics of book layout, or steering an aggressively independent route to self-publishing. Of course, that's a stereotype, but I think there's a pinch of truth here — just look at the mess many of them made when they first started building eBooks.

"This is how we make books. This is how we always made books. This is how books will always be made. There is a reason for this."

I exaggerate to illustrate a point, but typesetters who explain in blogs and in print how books should be laid out often come across as having this attitude. This can appear arrogant, yet for the most part, you should pay very close attention to what traditional typesetters say, because their norms come from centuries of producing books and learning what works and what does not. However, most typographic conventions are left over from the days not so long ago when typesetting meant arranging blocks of metal. In those days, producing crisp images was hard work. You've probably seen books yourself — biographies or modern history books, for example — where photographs and illustrations are separated onto special glossy paper. These images are printed separately using different paper stock and bound into the book later. We'll see why later in the topic about DOT GAIN [p242].

That limitation does not apply to you. At the point in the process where the printer puts ink onto the paper of your paperback, your PDF has been simplified into a series of dots. A human printer (rather than the machine) would say it's been RASTERIZED. The printing machine could be printing a letter 'T', or it could be printing one of the naughtier bits of a nude painting. The printing machine doesn't know or care — it's just dots.

If you are like me and have been on this earth for a few decades, then most of the books you will have read will have been designed with the mindset that illustrations are difficult and expensive to produce. In this book I frequently advise you to go look through your bookshelf and library to see how other books approach layout. This is the one area where this approach could let you down. Let your imagination soar because your Createspace book can freely intermingle text and illustrations of all sizes.

Ideas for images: fiction

- A logo for your publishing imprint. Place it toward the bottom of your title page (in the front matter).
- A photograph of you, the author. Place at the back.
- The front covers of your other books in an 'other books by the author' section. Place at the back.
- Use images to make fancy chapter headings. For example, if you've written a children's book set in the medieval period — princesses, knights, and courtly intrigue — you might have a knight presenting

sword and shield and have the chapter number emblazoned on the shield.

- Use images to make fancy PULL QUOTES and text boxes. (Pull quotes are excerpts or summaries from your text that are set in a larger font and designed to stand out. They are very common in magazines.) Suppose you have a 30s noir detective feel for your story — with a hardboiled detective in the mold of Philip Marlowe. You might feel the cynical but witty sayings of your detective are one of your book's strengths. How about this? Start each new chapter on a facing page. Have the chapter number and chapter title at top-right of the page. Place a small silhouette at bottom-left of an image that fits the theme: man in hat and trenchcoat slouching against an old-fashioned lamppost, or a fancy 1930s car, a blood splatter, or a femme fatale in 30s dress complete with furs. Start the text for each chapter on a facing page. That leaves a blank page between the chapter title page and the chapter text. Instead of leaving that blank, find an image of an art deco frame from a royalty-free image site such as shutterstock.com or fotolia.com. In your graphics editing software, place a quote from your detective inside the art deco frame using a titling font, and set the whole thing in dark gray to add visual interest. Place the frame quote centered on the blank page a third of the way down.
- Use images as fancy dropcaps [see p208]
- Maps and diagrams.
- Letters, scrolls etc.
- Fake newspapers. Remember those old black and white movies where the printing presses roll and the front page of the newspaper hits center screen with a headline about our movie hero? It's a well-used device for a lot of genre fiction. Remember Captain Kirk and his captain's log? You can have futuristic newsfeeds, status reports from the starship's main computer, typed up reports from the 1930s secret police, graffiti carved into the walls of the medieval castle/ cathedral. You can still do all these things using text rather than creating an image. But if you can produce the image well (or can get someone to do this for you) it can lift your book up to make it something special.
- Typographer's ornaments. This covers a wide variety of fiddly, flowery and fancy lines, borders and symbols. They go by a variety of names, which is really not important, so we'll call them all *ornaments*. Their main purpose is to divide sections of text and to frame titles. They are there to do a job, but they are also there to look stylish. They're so important that there's whole section on them shortly.

Ideas for images: non-fiction

- *All those ideas above for fiction are applicable to your non-fiction too.*
- *Some forms of non-fiction can be dry, especially how-to advice books, which can become a series of bullet points if you're not careful (rather like the book you're reading now; oh dear!). Images and other typographic flash (such as text boxes and quotes) can break up the bullet points to add visual interest.*
- Photographs for your travelogue or autobiography. There's no need to group photos together as you used to with old-fashioned books. Place the images alongside the text that relates to that image. Wrap the text around the image if it's small.
- Icons. Think of the idiot's guide, dummy's guide and similar book ranges. A magnifying glass might mean 'a closer look'. A bomb symbol in a triangular road sign might mean 'warning!'
- Create custom-designed text boxes in a graphics application (e.g. GIMP or Photoshop) that combine an icon with text. For example here's one I created for a Kindle book, but the idea works as well with a print book.

Take this opportunity to type your thoughts as notes on your Kindle, or just use good old-fashioned pen and paper.

Figure 42: An example of an icon & textbox as an inserted image

- Diagrams. Sometimes your text explains what you're trying to put across without the need for a diagram. But mixing images with text helps to spread the load in the reader's mind and makes the reading experience easier and more effective. I'm doing that in this book with the screenshots. With some of them I thought to myself: 'The description in the text is perfectly clear; I don't need a screenshot.' Sometimes one of the other voices in my head would reply: 'Yes, but there is too much straight text here. We need to break it up.' And so I went to the trouble of creating a screenshot anyway.

Images in eBooks

The image ideas for paperbacks almost all translate very nicely to eBooks in theory... but only when the image works as you intend! Images in eBooks are currently a dangerous business. Test very thoroughly and be extremely suspicious of most of the guidance you can find on the internet about how to place images in eBooks, because much of this guidance is inaccurate, outdated, or dangerously misleading.

For many of the images we've looked at with paperbacks, you will want the image to SCALE in the eBook. An image used as a chapter header, for example, might look superb in an old 600 pixel x 800 pixel eReader. But open that same book in a large HD tablet and that image now looks far too small. Or it might not, as some readers in some situations decide your image is too small and so blow it up. It might now be too big! And blown up images will certainly look blurry.

The answer would appear to be scaling. So for our example of an image used for a chapter heading, you might try to set the width of the graphic to be 65% of the page width.

In some cases you might be able to replace your png, jpg or gif image with a true vector graphic and scale using an svg wrapper (many typographer's ornaments are available as vector images — if you have Adobe Photoshop, you can convert ornamental glyphs available in some typefaces into vector graphics). You might keep your image as a jpg/png or gif (in other words as a raster image) and then scale anyway inside an svg wrapper. Or you might follow Amazon's current publishing guidelines for Kindle books and scale by setting a percentage value for the width/height attribute of your tags.

However, none of these scaling techniques gives consistently good results across all devices. Maybe one day I'll write a guide on how to use images in eBooks, but for now, make sure you test eBook images across a wide variety of devices and settings, and avoid using images in situations where both scaling and crispness are critical, such as chapter headings.

In some cases, scaling is not as important as crispness. For example, where I've used an image as a section divider for Kindles. Even with a true vector image, many kindles render them with jagged edges. Scaling raster images is no better. I've come to the conclusion that it's better to set the width and height of section divider images to pixel values and insert the images at 300dpi as Amazon tells us to. The result will not scale, but will look sharp across all devices.

Come back in a decade and you will find the eBook image scaling problems of late-2013 have all gone away. But for now, tread carefully because image support is brittle.

Typographer's Ornaments Revisited

We left the ornaments alone just a few pages ago after saying that the purpose of these lines, borders and symbols is to divide sections of text and to frame titles.

It's time to see some in action...

Chapter 7

L OREM IPSUM DOLOR SIT amet, consectetur adipisicing elit, sed do eiusmod tempor incididunt ut labore et dolore magna aliqua. Ut enim ad minim veniam, quis nostrud exercitation ullamco laboris nisi ut aliquip ex ea commodo consequat. Duis aute irure dolor in reprehenderit in voluptate velit esse cillum dolore eu fugiat nulla pariatur.

Excepteur sint occaecat cupidatat non proident, sunt in culpa qui officia deserunt mollit anim id est laborum.

Commentary

In this example we have an ornament below the chapter heading and at the end of the chapter (which would more normally last several pages). By the way, it's okay to refer to the ornament as a squiggly line. I hope so, anyway, because that's what I do. The effect is slightly old fashioned, somewhat ornate, but not overly so. This isn't right for a fast-paced gritty spy novel with fast men, loose cars, and dashing women (or some other arrangement of those adjectives). But for a historical adventure, modern romance or literary novel this could work well.

The fonts are Adobe Garamond Pro for the chapter title and drop cap, and Adobe Caslon Pro for the body set at 10 point with 1 point leading (i.e. the paragraph is set to 'at least 11 pt'). Alternative fonts that work well and you should have are Garamond instead of Adobe's Garamond Pro and Times New Roman for the body (a font that I feel is unfairly maligned). I would set more leading if I used Times New Roman, but this is the sort of thing you need to try for yourself by creating a private test project in Createspace and printing yourself a book with various layout options. (I know I keep repeating this; that's because I really want you to do it).

Now, a little more about that squiggly line. Where does the image come from?

A great way to pick up typographic ornaments is from a royalty free image site such as Shutterstock.com or Fotolia.com. Artists produce sheets of several ornaments per sheet and you pay a few dollars for the right to use them. Most of these will be vector graphics. If you don't have software to size vector graphics, you can always pick up a free vector graphics package such as Inkscape, and then save the images in png or jpg format. Once you've bought the images, they are yours to use for life, royalty free, so long as you credit the artist on your copyright page.

There are also plenty of royalty-free images provided by Microsoft as part of their Microsoft Office clip art (which you can access using INSERT | CLIP ART). Some of these images are very high quality and many symbols are vector artwork. To be honest I find them mostly applicable to non-fiction — especially for the corporate world — and are also great to liven up a blog post.

For paperbacks, using clip art or other royalty-free images works well. No problem. But most readers of this book will also want to produce eBooks, and will probably sell more eBooks than paperbacks. And with the eBook version we hit a problem: as I write this late-2013, there simply isn't an acceptable way to present images of this type. Sure, there are many techniques we can use, but every single one is riddled with compromise. See the next text box for the details...

What I've used in my example for the squiggly ornament is not a graphic at all, but a glyph typed on my keyboard. (A glyph is character or symbol defined in a font). What you might not realize is that you also have fonts with fancy glyphs such as this. What you also might not realize is that the glyphs in your TrueType and OpenType fonts (which is very nearly all of them) aren't defined as a series of pixels but are actually vector graphics. All the words you are reading on this page, whether in the paperback or the eBook edition, were defined on a font file as vector graphics. In terms of the way its curves and lines are defined, there's no difference between a symbol glyph defined as part of a font and a vector graphic for a similar symbol that you might acquire from Shutterstock.com.

Where there is a difference is the way in which the character is stored and displayed in Word, in the PDF file, in your eBook, and most importantly with your eBook reader. That symbol (〜) is part of the Minion Pro font, which most of you will have. Because the symbol is treated as any other character, it will always look sharp and will scale predictably.

To see which symbols you have access to, open up INSERT | SYMBOL in Word.

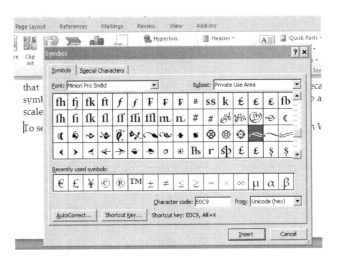

Figure 43: Inserting symbols for use as ornaments.

Here I've picked my squiggly line symbol. Like many of the ornamental glyphs, it's so wide that it has been clipped in the square box that you see here in Word. Note that I've had to select the font I want from the drop-down menu at the top-left of the box.

Make sure the box at the bottom-right is set to 'Unicode' or else you won't see all the glyphs. Unicode is an international standard that defines code numbers (called code points) for every character you can think of. I don't just mean the Latin alphabet and a few umlauts and accents; I mean Thai, Korean, Arabic, Hebrew and many other character systems.

Just because a character has an internationally agreed code number, that doesn't help you unless you have a font that defines how a glyph with that code number should look. Microsoft, Apple, Amazon (amongst others) have defined fonts with thousands or tens of thousands of characters in order to support a good chunk of the Unicode character set. Windows is the stand out winner here with the 'Arial Unicode MS' font. I confess I haven't counted them myself, but I've read this font has over 50,000 glyphs defined. With Macs try the Minion Pro font.

Webdings and Wingdings are properly defined vector graphics fonts too, which means that if you pick a character and scale it up, it will remain crisp. The downside is that these fonts mostly don't follow the Unicode standard and so won't translate reliably to eBooks (though you could capture the webding as an image and use that. With Photoshop you can type a character from any font and convert it to a vector graphic, or you could simply capture a screen shot of your character).

Here's a little selection from Webdings and Wingdings that might look good in your book:

Typographic ornaments in eBooks

As of late-2013, every approach you take here is riddled with compromise.

This is not true for web browsers and the fundamental structure of an eBook is a web page inside a wrapper that tells the eReader how the book fits together. So I expect this will eventually sort itself out for eBooks. You can always contact me on my webpage to find out the latest situation.

Riddled with compromise: that's a bold statement. Why do I say that?

The fundamental problem is that with eBooks you need to scale your ornaments (and other images). Go back two years and eInk eReaders such as the Kindle and Nook had a screen size of 600 pixels by 800 pixels. You could size your ornament to be, say, 160 pixels, stating that width in your tag and your ornament would look crisp and perfectly sized (so long as the human reader didn't do something awkward, such as read in landscape mode).

Now read that same book on a Kindle Fire HD 8.9" or an iPad4 retina display and what happens? The number of pixels on the screen has gone up enormously. What used to fit across the page nicely at 160 pixels now looks tiny. It looks wrong. It looks like the publisher doesn't know how to make eBooks and is foisting poorly produced eBooks on a gullible reading public. Yes, really, some readers are quick to condemn self-publishers and this gives them ammunition.

So what to do? Here are some things you can try.

Don't use ornaments at all in the ebook. Use a replacement such as tilda (~) or asterisk, for example, use a horizontal line (the <hr/> tag) or abandon the idea altogether.

Use a Unicode character. The problem here is that older readers (approximately pre-2010) might not display the character, though with Kindles you could use media queries to display an alternative. Also, Kobo readers are a problem because some fonts on the Kobo have little or no Unicode support, and the Kobo isn't clever enough to know that if a glyph isn't defined in the current font, that it should go find the glyph from a fall back font where it is defined.

If you are editing the html eBook code yourself, set scaling inside your tag. For example, width = "28%" height = auto. This is what Amazon currently recommends for Kindle books. Unfortunately, it doesn't work in all situations (though rarely – this can defeat Kindle Reader for PC) and the resulting image will be jagged, not crisp.

If you are editing the html eBook yourself, set the image inside an svg wrapper and scale that way. The result is never going to be crisp if you scale a jpg. Older readers (approximately pre-2010) won't support the svg wrapper. Even if you have a true vector graphic inside the svg wrapper, the results are often disappointing. For example iBooks on my iPad 4 will scale beautifully. The same book on my Nook Glow will not.

Make your image large enough that it looks good on a 600x800 eInk eReader, but also looks good shrunk down on an HD tablet. Of course, if future tablets or other devices are produced with even more pixels, then your image will shrink even further.

Come back in ten years, when there will probably be far more elegant solutions available ☺.

A few pages earlier, when I gave an example chapter using ornaments to give a slightly formal layout, I said it wasn't what I'd use for a spy thriller. So let's repeat the exercise with a Cold War spy thriller.

CHAPTER 7

LOREM IPSUM DOLOR SIT amet, consectetur adipisicing elit, sed do eiusmod tempor incididunt ut labore et dolore magna aliqua. Ut enim ad minim veniam, quis nostrud exercitation ullamco laboris nisi ut aliquip ex ea commodo consequat. Duis aute irure dolor in reprehenderit in voluptate velit esse cillum dolore eu fugiat nulla pariatur.

Excepteur sint occaecat cupidatat non proident, sunt in culpa qui officia deserunt mollit anim id est laborum.

LOREM IPSUM DOLOR SIT amet, consectetur adipisicing elit, sed do eiusmod tempor incididunt ut labore et dolore magna aliqua. Ut enim ad minim veniam, quis nostrud exercitation ullamco laboris nisi ut aliquip ex ea commodo consequat. Duis aute irure dolor in reprehenderit in voluptate velit esse cillum dolore eu fugiat nulla pariatur.

Excepteur sint occaecat cupidatat non proident, sunt in culpa qui officia deserunt mollit anim id est laborum.

Commentary

For fonts, this time I've used fonts you should have yourself: Verdana for the header, Palatino Linotype for the body (10 point with paragraphs set to 'at least 14 pt') and Arial Unicode MS for the hammer and sickle glyph. I've set the chapter header and the symbols to a dark gray color, which can be a simple but useful technique that translates well to eBooks if you handle the code yourself (set CSS styling to color: gray;).

The hammer and sickle symbol looks overdone twice on the same page but will look better in a real book with larger gaps between scene breaks. I set the font size for the symbol to 30 pt for use as a scene break character and to 40pt to terminate a chapter.

Font sizes: ultimate flexibility.

Remember I said earlier that all the characters you type in Microsoft Word are really defined as vector graphics?

That means the font size dropdown in Word gives *suggested* font sizes and that's all they are. You can use whatever font size you like. Those hammer and sickle symbols in my example are 30pt and 40pt, yet the only nearby sizes in the font size box are: 28pt, 36pt and 48pt. To get other sizes, click into the font size box and type in the number you want.

And you don't have to stick to whole numbers! If you are reading the paperback edition of this book, the body text is set in Palatino Linotype at 9.5pt size. That 9.5pt is not a 'faux' font size that doesn't look as good as a 'proper' font size. It is just as crisp, and every bit as valid as 9pt and 10pt.

When I first used Microsoft Word on the very first Apple Macs, fonts were defined as an array of dots. You had to stick to the font sizes offered. Those days are long past.

The horizontal line at the top of our Cold War example is an option in the borders and shading part of the Paragraph menu. I set the horizontal line to not go across the entire width of the page by styling the paragraph that contains the line to have a left and right margin.

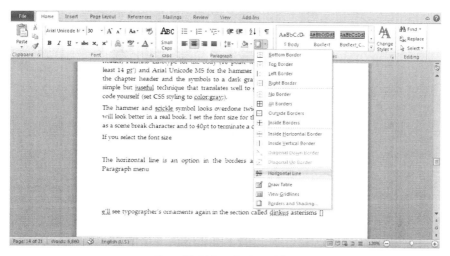

Figure 44: Adding a horizontal line.

I've not written a Cold War spy thriller (not yet, it does sound fun, though) but I have used the hammer and sickle technique with a supernatural thriller I published that featured werewolves as the dark threat. Instead of a hammer and sickle glyph I used this image (copyright Sushkonastya) that I picked up from fotolia.com

Figure 45: A typographic werewolf!

For the eBook I tried every option on a wide range of physical devices. In the end, even though the werewolf image was a vector graphic and I had originally scaled it using an svg wrapper, I decided the best approach was to abandon svg for now and set it as a 300dpi jpg scaled using width ="18%" in the tag.

We've covered a lot of ground here. Hopefully I've sparked your imagination and given you some tools to make your ideas appear in print. If I've succeeded then now would be a good time to go look through your library and see how other people have used images to enhance book design.

We'll see typographer's ornaments again in the section called DINKUS ASTERISMS [p183]

COLOR IMAGES, BLEED AND FULL PAGE IMAGES

I need to make you aware of a technical point here.

- Createspace can print full color as well as black and white. The printing costs for color is significantly higher.
- Createspace can print full bleed as well as pages with a margin around every edge of the page. You have to choose one or the other approach for every page in the book.

Most books have an invisible border around the edges — you must not print in this area. With any document in Word, if you try to print something right at the edge of the page, Word will refuse to print, telling you that the document content is 'outside the printable area'. We will cover margins later in the book, but this is how most of your books will work too. There is a minimum margin you must set around all four edges of the page. Createspace will not let you print outside of this 'printable area'.

I'm writing this section in Bedford Central Library. I can see three books on the shelf beside me that print the other way — full bleed. One is a book on British Wildlife. There are full color wildlife photographs on many of the pages, and the photos extend all the way to the edge of the page. The other books are one on gardening and one a reference to British mushrooms and toadstools. You can probably imagine the wealth of photography inside and the use of layers and borders to separate the various elements on the page so your eyes are subtly guided where to look so that you can make sense of the content. A lot of design work has gone into these books.

Every other book I've pulled off the shelf is printed the other way: there is an invisible blank border around the edge of the page where nothing is printed. Some of these books are heavy in color illustrations, such as the one on 1940s fashion, but they are not full bleed.

At one level, to make a book using full bleed pages is simple. All you need to do is set your page size to be 0.125" wider and 0.25" taller. Set the margins for your text as if the page sized were normal, but allow images to extend all the way to the edge of the page. The extra page size is called the BLEED, and you need to use it all to guard against slight inaccuracy when the paper sheets are trimmed.

If you're wondering why the bleed size appears to be uneven, it is because you need bleed at the top of the page and at the bottom, but you only need bleed on the outer edge of the page, not the inner. This does mean that there will be a band at the center of the book where your images do not go. Currently that minimum band is 0.75" for Createspace and 0.125" for Lightning Source.

So it's technically not too challenging to do full bleed, but if you were thinking that's what you want for your book, do take a look at commercial books with full-bleed pages. There's probably a lot of design experience and flair gone into that book. Could you design pages as well as that? My premise for this book is that armed with Microsoft Word and a willingness to learn, you can deliver most kinds of books through Createspace and make them look good enough for you to be proud of. Full-bleed books rich with illustrations are not 'most kinds of books'. You might find this too challenging and need help from a professional typesetter.

HOW TO INSERT IMAGES

Preparation: image file type and resolution

Common image file types are jpg, png, and tiff. They will all work fine, so long as you keep jpgs to maximum file quality. The file type that can cause problems are gifs because gifs have a limited number of colors. They can be great for line art (*line art* means images with a limited number of colors, of which black and white springs to mind — and I do mean black and white, not a wide range of subtle shades of gray.)

A minimum resolution of 300dpi or 300ppi for images is required by Createspace and any other printer. If crispness of image is not vital to you, then I would say you can go down to 200dpi/ppi without much concern. Much lower than 200dpi and your image will start to look seriously bad, and Createspace might refuse to print your book.

The terms dpi and ppi mean dots per inch and pixels per inch respectively. The higher the value the sharper the image. We'll come across those terms later, including how you can to some degree fake a higher dpi/ppi than is really there [see p 178]. The terms ppi and dpi don't actually mean quite the same thing, and there are some people in the world to whom the distinction is genuinely important. However, don't let anyone browbeat you into thinking the distinction has any relevance with regard to formatting a pdf file to upload to Createspace. In our context, the two terms are synonymous, and from here I will use the two terms interchangeably.

Colorspace and color gamut

If you delve into the Createspace community forums you will come across the term COLORSPACE. If you choose to buy Adobe Acrobat, you will come across the term there too. Colorspace refers to the way in which color is described, and all image files will contain. If you thought that blue was blue was blue, then you could get a serious shock if you start looking online and learn about colorspaces and color gamuts.

I started writing an explanation of these terms but thought better of it. Instead, I've separated out some extras details in PART 7 – ADVANCED TOPIC UNDER THE HEADING ADVANCED COLORSPACES AND DOT GAIN [p 242] What I'm setting out here are out the key things you might need, without going into the detail that 99.9% of people simply don't need to know.

Consider these points:

- Under Windows you can easily tell a colorspace for an image by right-clicking the image in File Explorer (the app you use in Windows to move files around your computer) and inspecting the file properties.
- Unless you are dealing with an artist, almost every color image you will encounter will be in a colorspace called sRGB. Createspace print these just fine. Leave them alone.
- Even if you are printing a black and white book, if your image is in color, leave it alone. If you upload a PDF with color images, Createspace will happily print them in black and white.
- Some people have in the past reported slight improvements by converting color images to black and white and manipulating them before uploading. Unless you're an expert, I think you're more likely to do harm than good with this, but that brings me to the next point.
- The only way to know how an image will appear in the finished book is... You already know the answer! Print a dummy version of your book with the various approaches and see what works best. You may find that different images in the same book each work best with a slightly different approach.
- You might come across an image in the CMYK colorspace, almost certainly from a graphic artist. This will print fine, but do not change it to sRGB! Leave well alone. Only high grade graphics apps will allow you to manipulate CMYK images (GIMP, Paint.net and Adobe Elements are examples of software that do not allow editing of CMYK). So bear in mind that if you contract with a graphic artist to supply images, if you get CMYK back then they are read-only for you unless you have a top-notch graphics app such as Adobe Photoshop.

What you see is NOT what you get

The way a color image on a computer screen gets into your eye (colored lights are added together) is the complete reverse of how the same image gets into your eye on a color printed page (ink absorbs ambient light and the mix of colored light reflected back is what we perceive as color). The same is true for black and white and grayscale, and the difference is more pronounced with some colorspaces than others, especially the CMYK colorspace.

The upshot is that when you look at your computer screen, you can only ever get an approximate idea of how an image will look in print. You need to print a proof copy and examine the evidence.

In particular, black and white and grayscale images that look ideal on the printed page will often look too dark on your computer monitor.

With our preliminaries out of the way, here are the steps to follow to insert images...

1. Keep the images separately in a safe place, then insert them

Keep your images in a safe place as separate image files. If you have a large number of images (such as in the book you're reading) it will make your life much easier to adopt a naming convention too — such as embedding the topic inside the filename.

Even if you're taking screenshots, it's best to save as a file and then insert the file rather than copy and paste directly from the clipboard. Otherwise, if you need manipulation and want to go back a step, you will not have an original to go back to. Also, you will need screenshots as separate files if you are going to build an eBook.

I keep a safe backup of the images in their original state in a separate place from the images I manipulate for the printed book. If you are going to use the same images in an eBook, you will need several different versions of each image.

Insert your images so that the image is embedded inside your Word file. There is an alternative of linking to the image file rather than embedding it. The only advantage to linking is if you expect to change image files that are used in many places. In other respects, linking is a bad idea because it's easy to break your Word file when you move it from one location to another.

2. Set gridlines on

It's easy when placing images to accidentally place the image outside of the PRINTABLE AREA. The printable area is the space on the page inside the margins you set in Page Setup [see p77]. It isn't normally possible to add text outside of your printable area even if you try. With images, it's dangerously easy.

To save yourself having to redo your image placement after accidentally placing images into the margins, turn on gridlines (VIEW | GRIDLINES).

You should now see a grid as in the screenshot.

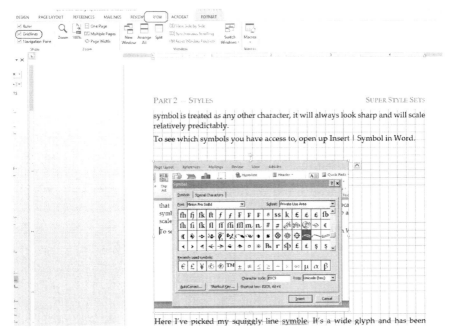

Figure 46: Placing an image using gridlines

Sometimes, though, nothing happens. No matter how hard you press the mouse button, the gridlines don't appear. The answer is to correct the values in the Drawing Grid Dialog (PAGE LAYOUT| ALIGN | GRID SETTINGS...). You will find some blank values. Fill in the empty values as in the screenshot below.

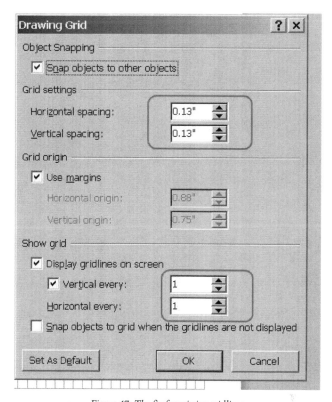

Figure 47: The fix for missing gridlines

3. Use the size and position menu to place the image

In addition to sizing your image, the SIZE AND POSITION dialog gives you fine control over where your image appears on the page and how text wraps around it. If you've used images in Word, I'm sure you will at some point have seen the dialog window below.

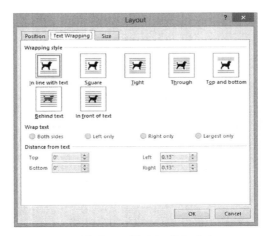

Figure 48: The Size and Position dialog for images

It's a little confusing as its naming is not consistent. You can bring up this dialog in Word 2013 by:

- Right clicking on the image and picking 'Size and Position...'
- Left Click on the image, and then from the Ribbon, FORMAT I Position I More Layout Options...
- Left Click on the image, and then from the Ribbon, FORMAT I Wrap Text I More Layout Options...
- Left Click on the image. Left click on the Layout Options square that appears alongside the image. Select 'See more...'

The Position tab of the dialog looks like this

Figure 49: Positioning images

There are a lot of controls here. And you will find them all explained by Microsoft in Word Help. I'm not going to parrot what Microsoft has already written. Instead, I'll start by telling you what you need to know to produce large centered images, and then move to introduce floating text around your image.

Centering an image

You have two approaches here: setting the text wrapping to 'In line with text' or 'Top and bottom'. If you want to keep the image in the same place as a particular paragraph, using In Line with text is slightly easier.

The **In line with text** wrapping option treats your image as a large character in paragraph of text. Occasionally this is actually what you need for special effects but for large centered images (such as the screenshots in this book) you don't want to mingle text with images like that.

Instead, hit the Return key to add a blank line, make sure the cursor is on the blank line before inserting your picture.

To center your image, set the paragraph that contains the image to a centered style. Now, be careful with this. If your default paragraph style has a first line indent (as is the norm with fiction) then your image will not be at true center, it will be shifted to the right by the amount of your first line indent. Not what you want! So use a centered style with first-line indent set to zero.

The *In Line with text* approach has the advantage of keeping things simple. The image's position is set by the paragraph style that contains it. The image has no anchor, and the Position tab of the Size and Position dialog is grayed out (meaning you cannot enter any values here).

The alternative approach is to insert the image where you want on the page and use the **Top and bottom** wrapping option. This makes text appear above and below the image (as you would expect) and links the image to the place where you inserted it. If you click on the image, an anchor shows on the page. Many of the image position options define themselves in relation to this anchor. In the screenshot of the Position dialog I've just shown you, the Vertical alignment is set to 'Absolute position: 0in. below paragraph'. The paragraph it refers to is the one with that little icon symbol. To move the image, move the anchor.

To center the image, set the horizontal alignment to center.

If you change the wrapping or anchor position, Word will often reset the Position settings, so when you have images in your document, carry out a final check of the image positions before printing your proof. Sometimes I find the images have reset and are no longer truly centered.

Have a go yourself now!

Make a copy of a Word document with a few pages of text, insert a few images and start playing with the options. You'll be an expert before you know it.

Floating text around images

By this I mean 'all the other text wrapping options'. Really, they work the same as the Top and Bottom that we've just seen except that the text appears in the same lines as the image.

For the paperback edition, I've done just this with the book reading figure to the right.

I clicked at the start of the paragraph above that starts 'By this I mean...'. And inserted my image. It was too large and so I resized it. Then I changed the wrapping type to **square**.

The image jumped down the page to the wrong place and so too did the anchor!

That was easily fixed. I dragged the anchor back to the correct paragraph. Then I opened the Size and Position dialog and set the following:

Horizontal: Alignment right relative to column

Vertical: Absolute alignment 0inch relative to paragraph

In the **Options** I made sure that Move object with text was ticked (turned on).

Move object with text... or not?

You will see options to keep the image with text or in an absolute position on the page. Both work as described, but there is no easy answer to suggest which is best. I'm afraid it depends on the context and the changes you make to your book after you insert the image. Setting the image to move with text has the advantage of keeping the image next to the right piece of text. However, after changes to your book, that might leave the page layout looking poor. Keeping the image in the same place on the page can look good in terms of layout, but the text that refers to the image might have drifted several pages away by the time you've finished the book.

Whichever approach you take, I suggest that as one of the final checks for your document, reassess the layout for every image. If you have a lot of images, chances are you will need to place some of them again at the end.

Image placement horrors ... and their solutions.

Wrapping ... relative positioning ... anchors ... there is a lot to learn about image placement and a lot to go wrong. If your images rebel and don't go where you want, you won't be the only one to have cursed Word for the same reasons. Luckily that means there is a lot of support videos and discussions online on this topic. Here are some things to check first:

Word 2013 changed the default text wrapping settings for inserting images. The default changed from 'In Line with text' to 'Top and bottom'. So if you are used to a certain way of handling images, this may be why you are not getting the same results.

In line with text means the image is treated as a (big) character inside a paragraph of text. If you set the paragraph line spacing after you inserted the image, you might make the line height too short to display the image, which will seem to disappear.

If your image jumps to the wrong page, and you can't explain why, bring up the Size and Position dialog (by right clicking on the image) and look at the Position tab. Look at the page to see where the image anchor is actually located (Note that *In Line with Text* images don't have an anchor). This should explain why your image has jumped.

4. How to set captions

Right click on the image and select 'insert caption'. You can get this from the References part of the Ribbon too. The book you are reading has screenshots and sometimes I want to refer to a specific screenshot to remind myself how to do something. Yes, I do read my own book! For my book, captions with figure numbers are very useful. The table of figures at the front of the book is auto-generated by Word by clicking on 'table of figures' from the References menu on the Ribbon.

For a lot of other books, figure numbers aren't appropriate in the caption (e.g. an illustrated children's book). You can't insert a caption without including a figure number. You don't need to, though. Insert the caption with the figure and then immediately click on the caption, which allows you to edit the text. Simply delete the figure number and leave the rest. If only everything in life were so easy!

Captions and eBooks

There is no reliable way to make a caption appear sharp and in the correct place next to an image in an eBook with reflowable text. The closest I have seen is if you style the code yourself and embed the text in the same block as the image like this:

```
<p class="imgCentred">
    <img alt="Fables" height="350"
    src="../Images/Fables_s.jpg" width="244" />
    <br /><i>Cover art by Dean Harkness</i>
</p>
```

This often works, especially for smaller images, but if the eReader device really wants to, it will put the caption on the next page anyway. Even setting a paragraph style with page-break-inside:avoid doesn't prevent this.

The only way to be sure of the placement of the caption is to expand the image canvas down in your graphics software and type in the caption as a part of the image. This will put the caption the right place but the caption text will never look as sharp as the surrounding text.

5. Using frames, shadows and special effects

Don't use Word for this!

You can get some good effects in Word that can look good on screen and when you print directly from Word, but when creating the PDF these don't always come across well.

If I apply borders or text shadows to images, I do so in a separate application, such as Photoshop or GIMP, make sure to flatten the image (there will be a command in your app to do this), and then insert the new image into Word.

HOW MICROSOFT WORD
RUINS YOUR IMAGES
PART#2

I summarized earlier how Word has an annoying tendency to mess up your images if you're running the Windows operating system. Turn back to [p144] if you need to refresh your memory.

Mac users have an easier time. If you're running MacOS X Leopard (2007) or later, then Apple lets you save as a high resolution PDF with the built-in Save to PDF facility. I believe Mac users will still face the automatic downgrading of images within Word to 199dpi unless you are at least at Word 2011, but I have to say I don't have Word 2008 on the Mac to confirm this.

Before we proceed, one reminder: for most self-publishers of fiction, printing images at 300dpi might be a nice-to-have but is not essential. If your only image in your book is your author picture, it may actually look better at 200dpi (No offence intended! Quite apart from other considerations, 300dpi can emphasize flaws in photography not shot to a professional standard).

If you're running Word under Windows, here's how you are affected.

Word 2003

Problems: if you move your image, resize your image, or save your file, all images will be reduced to a maximum of 200dpi. There's no built-in PDF export facility.

Solutions: get a third party PDF driver [see below] and try exporting to pdf before saving your Word document. Upgrade to a newer version (at least Word 2010).

Also: to avoid Word reducing image resolution below 200dpi, you need to set the right **Compression settings**. Follow the steps for Word 2007 below, although the **Compress Pictures** button will appear on the **Picture Toolbar** rather than on the Ribbon.

Word 2007

Problems: if you move your image, resize your image, or save your file, all images will be reduced to a maximum of 220dpi.

You can export to PDF from the File | Save As menu inside Word 2007. If that option isn't available, then you need to download an Office add-on from Microsoft. Google for '2007 Microsoft Office Add-in: Microsoft Save as PDF or XPS'. PDF export reduces image resolution to 200dpi.

Solutions: get a third party PDF driver [see below]. Upgrade to a newer version (at least Word 2010).

Also: to tell Word to keep images at the maximum resolution it will permit, before you start inserting images, carry out the following steps.

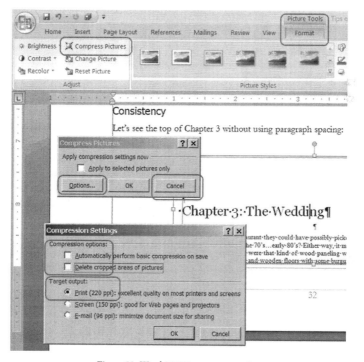

Figure 50: Word 2007 image-compression

- First click on any image to bring up the **Picture Tools** menu on the Ribbon.
- Click on **Compress Pictures** (on the Ribbon)
- Click Options...
- Match my settings in the **Compression Settings** dialog.
- **OK** the Compression Setting dialog

- But **Cancel** the Compress Pictures dialog. (This changes the options but doesn't then apply compression).

- It may seem strange to open up a window, only to cancel it, but if you don't check you've got the right Compression settings, you will reduce your image quality simply by saving the file.

That's not all. Sometimes, when you save as a new document file, Word decides to default back to compressing images again. In the **Save As...** dialog, there is a button called **Tools** at the bottom. Click on this, and then Compress Pictures... This brings up the Compression Settings dialog I've just shown you. You need to set the Target output the same as we've just seen in the screenshot above.

Word 2010 & 2013

Problems: Image resolution will be reduced in Word unless you tell Word not to. Word has PDF export capability but will always reduce image resolution to 200dpi.

Solutions: get a third party PDF driver [see below].

Also: To tell Word not to reduce image resolution, *before* you start inserting images, go to Word Options | Advanced | Image Size and Quality and set option to 'Do not compress images in file'. Congratulations – your image resolution is preserved.

Word Options are accessed from the File menu.

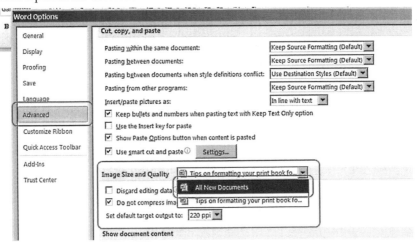

Figure 51: Word 2010 & 2013 image compression — problem solved!

Note that in the screenshot I have selected the option for 'All New Documents'. Otherwise, it will only apply to the current document and not when you save it as a new name.

Third-Party PDF drivers

Years ago when I was proud to be running a sparkly new copy of Word 2003, I tried out several third-party PDF drivers. I had problems with all of them, but did eventually get acceptable results. Fast forward to the present day and I now use Adobe Acrobat Pro to make my PDFs but there are still third-party PDF makers that act as printer drivers, except if you print to these add-ons, your document comes out as a pdf file rather than as ink or toner on your printer. Essentially this is what Mac owners have had provided by Apple ever since the version of OS X that came out in 2007.

I've listed third party PDF drivers that I've seen recommended by individuals I regard as credible. Please don't take this as an endorsement from me. Some printers (Lightning Source International, but not Createspace or Lulu) require the PDF of your interior to be in PDF/X format. From looking at the websites of these Windows PDF tools, none of them claim that capability. Adobe Acrobat Pro does produce PDF/X files , as do Macs anyway.

Microsoft — since Office 2007, Word has had a PDF export facility. The PDFs it produces look good to me with one exception: images are downgraded to 199dpi. This is still true of Office 2013. If you don't need high resolution images, this will work acceptably. If you do... too bad! You must use something else or upload a Word document rather than a PDF.

doPDF — Does the basic tasks well, including setting image dpi up to 1200dpi and flexible page sizes. Is free, but more facilities in a paid version (such as setting hyperlinks in your PDF file; all things that are useful in an office environment, but not useful for our use with Createspace).

Nitro Pro — Compares itself to Adobe Acrobat Pro for less than half the price tag ($120 last I looked). Does a lot more than simply create PDF files.

CutePDF Writer— the basic version that works as a simple printer driver is free. Like many other cheap PDF printer drivers, it doesn't actually create the PDF file itself, but is more of a wrapper for the freeware Postscript to PDF tools such as Ghostscript. There are Pro versions that let you do more but nothing necessary for printing to Createspace.

NovaPDF - Another PDF driver I've seen and heard recommended. Currently costs $40-$50 depending on which version you buy.

WORKING WITH IMAGES THAT AREN'T 300DPI

You can tell the actual resolution (i.e. how many dots per inch) of your images by loading your manuscript into the Interior Reviewer in Createspace. If your images aren't high enough resolution, it will tell you. If you click on the warning symbol at the top-right of the Interior Reviewer screen, it will tell you which images are causing the problem.

If Interior Reviewer is complaining about your low-resolution images, it might still let you publish. Look carefully at what Interior Reviewer is telling you. You can generally accept *warnings* but can't accept *errors*. The human Createspace reviewers (the next step after Interior Reviewer) might let you off with your warnings.

What if your image turns out to be only 96dpi? Or some other resolution where you know you should upload a higher resolution to Createspace/ Lulu but the original image file is not at the resolution you want?

That's what I faced in making this book; all the screenshots were captured at 96dpi. That's nowhere near enough quality for a print book and the eBook generally looks better with 150dpi. What then?

You have three options:

1. Don't use that image.
2. Resize the image: increase the resolution by shrinking the image.
3. Resize the image: shrink it as before, but then resample a larger version.

If you're going to resize, you need a proper graphics package. It doesn't have to be expensive, or even full-featured, but you do need the capability to resample properly. Adobe Photoshop and the more basic Photoshop Elements are popular graphic editing software that you pay for. But Gimp and Paint.net are free.

Gimp is sometimes called the *open-source Photoshop*. It is a fully featured package that is daunting for beginners but has a lot of free tutorials posted by Gimp users available online. Available for free and for Windows and Mac at www.gimp.org

Paint.Net is Windows-only and free. It is simpler that Gimp. Although it can't do as much in terms of creating images, that can be a blessing. It's easier to find your way around and quick to load up. Download from www.getpaint.net

I tend to use Paint.NET for book interiors because it is quick to load and run (I used it for the screenshots in the book you're reading). It hasn't nearly as many features as GIMP or Photoshop, but you don't need them for book interiors. All these graphics packages will have something like this Paint.NET **Resize Image** screen.

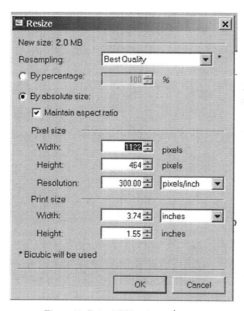

Figure 52: Paint.NET — Image | Resize

For GIMP, there is an **Image | Scale Image...**, which brings up a dialog very similar to the Paint.NET example. For GIMP users who want to change the print size without resampling use **Image | Print Size...** instead (this keeps the same number of dots in your image but increases or decrease the resolution — see next section for why you might want to do this).

Image basics... and image resizing

To understand resizing and resampling, I'll first explain some basics of image resolution. Suppose you have a black and white image that's 3 inches square, and is at a resolution of 100 dots per inch (100 dpi). That means the image is composed of a square 300 dots high and 300 across. Each dot is either black or white. Sometimes these dots are called *pixels*, and the resolution described as *pixels per inch* or ppi. Dots... pixels, they don't actually mean quite the same thing but for our purposes they do, and so I'm going to use them interchangeably.

Suppose we take another 3 inch square image, this time at 200dpi. This square is now 600 dots high and 600 wide (3in. x 200dpi = 600dots). There are twice as many dots in each direction and so the image is said to be a *higher resolution*. In fact there are four times as many dots in total in the image (600 x 600 = 360,000 dots; our first square had 300 x 300 = 90,000 dots).

Now, go back to our original 100dpi image: 300 dots high and 300 wide; 3 inches high and 3 wide. What we can do is shrink the image so it is 1 inch square. We still have our 300 dots, but we are shrinking each dot. Now we have a square that is 1 inch high and 300 dots high. By presenting our same dots in a smaller area, we have increased the resolution: our image is now 300dpi, and so Createspace will be happy. Whether you will be happy with the smaller image is something you need to decide. This is option-2.

Suppose it is vital that you must have your image at 3 inches square. In this case, you can take your shrunken 300dpi image and *resize* it. This is option-3.

To continue our example, we will take our 1 inch/ 300 dot square (300dpi) and tell Paint.NET, or whatever you are using, that you now want it to be 3 inches square. Notice that the Resize screen (above) mentions *resampling*. When Paint.NET resizes our image, it will keep the image at 300dpi. When we resize 1 inch (at 300dpi) and make it 3 inches (still at 300dpi) that means we must now have a square with height and width of *900 dots* (for a total of 810,000 dots).

To do this, your graphics package creates new dots. It uses clever resampling algorithms to keep the line of a curve smooth. It's very impressive. While technically you've just magicked an image that was originally 100dpi into a 300dpi image of the same dimensions, in practice it will never look as good as an image that had been 300dpi all the way. In our example, we started off with 90,000 dots and finished with 810,000 dots. Or to put it another way almost 90% of the dots in our resized image have been invented by Paint.NET, or whatever graphics package you are using.

Some images look better than others after this fraud; some look very obviously blurred. If your graphics package has a sharpening filter, that can help a little.

Part 6 — Details

Dinkus asterisms & section breaks • The final tidies • Do you need to upload a PDF? • Embedding fonts • Front matter • Adding blank pages at the end • Widows and orphans • Tables of Contents • Drop caps and small caps

Dinkus Asterisms, and
How Print and eBooks
are very Different

Typography sometimes uses bizarre terms such as here in the case of what I am going to call *section breaks*.

This is where you tell the reader that you're moving to a new scene by the visual cue of a gap between the scenes (in this context, I'm not using *section* in the sense we saw earlier with page numbers and headers). Sometimes this visual cue can be a blank line, but asterisks or other symbols may be used too. Now, I'm starting off by using the term 'scene break' loosely. You will probably already have a clear idea of what constitutes a scene. Like a play, we move to a new location or time and restart the narrative. Sometimes the restart is more gentle; we might use a blank line to indicate time passing; perhaps a character fell asleep and has awoken, or maybe they have been walking to a destination and you add a break to show time has passed and they are now at their destination.

There are other types of break too, such as the switching from narrative to the text of a letter being read or a song sung. What you choose to call these is up to you, but I will refer to all of them as section breaks.

Whether you choose to use a centered asterisk, or other character, or whether you leave your section breaks as a blank line is a matter of taste. However, consider these points:

- The most important factor is clarity.

- For a print book, if you know the section break would occur *at the bottom of the page* then you need to make this clear to the reader by adding centered asterisks or other characters. Otherwise the reader will not realize there has been a break and may get confused and then irritated.

- Be consistent with whatever approach you use.

- If in doubt, do whatever gives the clearest reading experience.

For myself, I tend to use a single centered asterisk for breaks that I consider a scene break. To set off letters being read and songs being sung within a scene, I use blank lines. With non-fiction, I also set off some elements with blank lines, such as that bulleted list above, and centered images. My definition of a scene break might not be yours. If you regularly format print and eBook versions of the same manuscript, I suggest you follow my approach because the rule that says you need to champion the clearest reading experience dictates that approach to section breaks. That's because if you produce an eBook...

You cannot tell how your eBook will look

Many traditional print books only put symbols into the section breaks when forced to (i.e. when the blank line would come at the bottom of the page and so would otherwise be invisible). But with eBooks this is simply not an option because you can *never* know where the section breaks will occur on the page. If your section breaks are blank lines then some readers *will miss them* because they *will* fall at the bottom of the page. That's poor formatting; don't do it!

Instead, use the centered asterisk (or other symbol) for all scene breaks. The only exception I normally make to this is where you break the narrative to quote from a letter or a song. That shouldn't be a problem anyway, because you can set your letter, song, poem, memory off in italics.

Notice I wrote *scene breaks*. This is where it can get tricky if you're going for special effects. If you have divided your chapter into a large number of small chunks (of a handful of lines), those asterisks in the section breaks can quickly become very intrusive. There's no simple answer to this, except to take the approach that gives the clearest reading experience to the largest number of readers.

My answer is sometimes to break my own default rule and ditch the asterisk on a scene by scene basis where a scene has many of these tiny chunks. It doesn't happen often, though. We're talking special effects such a scene where you are rapidly swapping between different viewpoint characters.

You can be adventurous with scene breaks and enhance the look of your book. You can also go too far and make your book look ridiculous.

For example, in this aside I've added a horizontal line above and below, a technique I've used in some non-fiction books to set off text from the main body.

You can make the text look even more distinct from the main body by changing the font or size, adding a left and right margin, and changing from black text to gray.

I've done all of the above in this aside. The horizontal lines come from selecting 'horizontal line' from the borders & shading button in the Paragraph section of the Ribbon.

The horizontal lines are easy to implement with your eBooks if you are doing your own CSS styling. The lines above would be implemented in the html code as

```
<hr/>
```

And the left and right margins for the line would come from your CSS stylesheet where you would add something like:

```
hr{2em 25%;}
```

You can also use images instead of asterisks for your separating characters. I laid out a collection of young adult stories (*Alien Legends*) with the conceit that stories were story spheres translated into human languages from an alien story collective called *The Repository of Imagination*. After each story was a wry comment from an alien repositarian. This was a fun book to work on and could be enhanced by a little design work. So I sourced an image I felt would make a good story sphere and inserted it between the text of each story and the repositarian's comment. To further distinguish comments from story text, I also put the end comment in italics. More than a few paragraphs of italics are difficult to read, but these comments were brief.

Finally, I had a few longer stories that had scene breaks within them. I took the story sphere and shrunk the image to make a scene break. And I could reuse exactly the same image and layout design for the Kindle and ePUB versions of the same book.

And here is my story sphere image. It's out of context here, but looks superb in *Alien Legends*.

I sourced the image as a vector graphic from Fotolia.com You pay a few dollars for the right to use the image, but have to acknowledge the artist, which is fair enough. This particular image is copyright Pulsar 75.

I've done something similar in using a double-headed axe for a David Gemmell high fantasy tribute anthology, the werewolf silhouette you saw earlier for a supernatural thriller, and a double right arrow glyph))➡ (which is Unicode code point 279F) in a collection of philosophical science fiction.

THE FINAL TIDIES

There are a few tidy-ups best left to the end because they fix problems that are very easy to slip in at any point — including during editing. I'm referring to little things like

- Double spaces between words (the least offensive of these manuscript naughties)
- A space between the period and the end of the paragraph.
- A mix of curly and not curly double and single quotes
- Curly quotes that *face the wrong way.*
- Other non-formatting details, such as being consistent with capitalization, hyphenation, and spelling out numbers or using numerals.

The cumulative effect of not tidying these can be a scrappy-looking print book. And that second point (extra spaces at the end of a paragraph) might sound trivial but can devastate the look of your eBook.

Luckily Microsoft Word has a superb tool for sorting these semi-automatically: **Find and Replace**.

Make a note to do these tidy-ups after your editing but before you do final copy editing.

The key to using Find and replace (which you can bring up with Ctrl + H) is to click the **More >>** button, and then **Special**. We did this earlier when talking about Smashwords and section breaks: there we searched for *section breaks* and replaced with *page breaks.*

I'm going to assume that all of the bullet items above are errors and need to be addressed. If you have a few locations where you have used this formatting deliberately (perhaps using multiple spaces to align text) then you'll have to think more carefully about your approach. If there are only a few cases, you might want to take a backup, do the global find and replaces I'm about to show, and then paste back in the saved versions for the sections you wish to preserve.

Let's look at this in action. If we press the **Show/Hide** button on the Ribbon we can reveal some of these manuscript naughties.

Figure 53: Show/hide

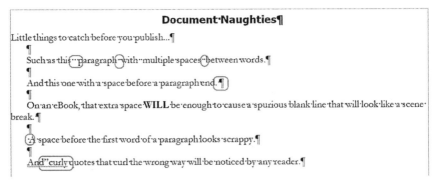

Figure 54: Document naughties!

The fixes in turn are:

- **Double spaces between words.** Type two spaces in the FIND box, and one space in the REPLACE box. Then REPLACE ALL. See how many are fixed. Keep replacing all until Word reports zero replacements.
- **A space between the period and the end of the paragraph.** Type a space following by a paragraph mark (from the **Special** list) in the FIND box, and a paragraph mark (without any spaces) in the REPLACE box. Then REPLACE ALL. See how many are fixed. Keep replacing all until Word reports zero replacements.
- **Starting the paragraph with a space.** I can't find a reliable way to eliminate these automatically. Take them out the hard way, by hand. Alternatively, copy the document to a text editor with RegEx capability as described in the box later in this section.
- **A mix of curly and not curly double and single quotes - setup autoformatting first** Before you do this, check you have **autoformat** and **autocorrect as you type** set to **Replace straight quotes with smart quotes**. In Word 2010 and newer you set this in file | options. In Word 2007, you set this through **Office Button** (the round thing at top-left) | **Word options** | **Proofing** | **Autocorrect options...** Word 2003 has the

same functionality but different routes in (look up *autocorrect* and *autoformat* in your Help).

- **A mix of curly and not curly double and single quotes - the fix** With your autoformatting set, type a double quote into FIND and a double quote into REPLACE, then REPLACE ALL. To get this quote character, simply press Shift + 2 — you don't need to mess around with inserting symbols or anything fancy. What Word will do is find any straight quote character, or curly quotes facing either direction, and change it to a curly quote (Microsoft call these *smart* quotes) curling in the right direction. *Magic!* I still get a thrill from this. I formatted quote marks the hard way before I realized I could do it in seconds; I hope someone reading these words is equally wowed. The same trick works for single quotes/ apostrophes.

- Curly quotes that *face the wrong way*. You get this if there isn't a space between a double quote and the preceding word at the point when Microsoft Word decides which way around to turn the curly quote. That missing space isn't as easy to spot as you might think. A curly quote facing the wrong way looks awful, though. So make sure you carry out a proper copyedit after you've done your automatic quote-curling. The fix is to put in the missing space. Delete the quote and reinsert it. Make a list of common culprits and search for them. Here's my list: 'em, 'erm, 'cause, 'er, 'ad, 'ave, 'is, 'im, 'ere, 'tis, 'til.

- On the topic of autoformatting — watch out for the situation where you have different people working on your manuscript with different autoformatting options in Word. Or where you work on more than one computer and have different settings on each. When I come to format manuscripts for clients, I often see a mix of straight and curly quotes, the result of the client writing the manuscript on different machines. It easy for authors to be blind to this but to a reviewer this can look extremely scruffy.

Tidying your document using regular expressions

Regular expressions (often shortened to 'RegEx') are a powerful search and replace tool often used by programmers. Unfortunately they aren't available in Word, but if you make eBook versions and get your hands dirty with html, then you will probably be using tools that do have RegEx, such as Notepad++ or Sigil.

RegEx allows you to do a few things that Word's find and replace cannot. In particular

^ +

Finds paragraphs that start with a blank space. Leave the 'replace' box empty and this will remove them automatically.

^[a-z]

Detects paragraphs that start with a lower case character (make sure to set case sensitivity on). This isn't foolproof, but is a good way to detect paragraphs that have been broken up by paragraph breaks that shouldn't be there.

We're talking here about paperbacks not eBooks. I only mention this because the RegEx I run when building eBooks sometimes throws up issues that I need to fix in the paperback edition.

My workflow is normally: lay out paperback in Word but don't publish until the eBook is built — strip out formatting and paste into Notepad++ to start building eBook — if my Notepad++ RegEx finds problems that apply to the paperback edition, I apply those fixes — finish off ePUB edition in Sigil — rework the ePUB edition for Kindle-specific formatting and run through Kindlegen to build the Kindle edition.

By the way. My last word on curly quotes. I did pick up a rumor at one point that Smashwords doesn't accept curly quotes, or mangles their formatting. This isn't quite true. I always use curly quotes with Smashwords and have had no problems getting through to the Premium Catalog.

Apparently, though, there are genuine problems with displaying curly quotes (and em-dashes) with the old Palm PDB format. You will get ugly 'nonsense' characters. You could replace em-dashes with hyphens and curly with straight quotes. But, to be brutally honest, you are not likely to sell many PDB-format books. When I used to upload Word documents to Smashwords, I turned off the option to produce PDB books. (Now I don't use Word documents at all with Smashwords. I upload ePUB files directly, which is a much tidier option.)

DO I REALLY NEED TO UPLOAD A PDF?

When I first produced POD books, there was no option here. All the print-on-demand suppliers I was aware of required you to supply them with a print-ready PDF. Lulu still does that but also provides a tool which can take your Word .doc file and converts it to PDF format for you to inspect and then pass back to Lulu if you're happy for them to print it. Recently, Createspace changed this by allowing you to upload .doc, .docx and .rtf to the Interior Reviewer.

Most writers are likely to be much more comfortable with Microsoft Word or Open Office than with software such as Adobe Acrobat that allows you to edit PDF files directly. So for Lulu to provide a PDF converter (which I've used and works very effectively) and Createspace to allow you to upload native Microsoft Word files, and widely supported rtf files, is an exciting step forward. After all, PDF is a format used by printers, not writers. It's about time that a print-on-demand service offered to writers used our formats.

I'm sure Createspace recognizes this and want to make their service as writer-friendly as they can.

All of this sounds like a big endorsement from me to ignore PDFs and send Createspace your Word files. I think it is worth you trying this out, but inspect the results very carefully. My reservation is that when I've sent .docx, .doc and .rtf files to the Interior Reviewer I found that it didn't understand my headers. It didn't seem to understand my alignment tabs. You shouldn't need to understand what alignment tabs are, but the Interior Reviewer should, and clearly doesn't. Image placement went haywire too. I'm confident all these teething problems will eventually be addressed, but if you upload anything other than PDF to Createspace, I would look at the results very carefully indeed.

Looking around the Createspace Community and elsewhere online to see how others fare with uploading files in formats other than PDF, I see many people with problems. If the results aren't good for you in .docx, try .doc, which may give different results. Look carefully for headers and footers, image placement, and blank pages inserted where you didn't expect them to be.

If uploading other file formats isn't working for you, check out some of the PDF add-ins around. I've listed a few in the section on Key Third Party Software on [p251].

I expect my working setup is slightly different to yours because most of the books I lay out are for publishers or other self-publishing authors. It isn't acceptable for me to give my clients a formatted .docx file and say 'try that — it might work, and there again, it might not'! I need to know for sure it will work first time with Createspace or any other printer, and that's why I always produce PDF files when I format books.

But whatever file format you upload, if you order a proof copy from Createspace, closely inspect it, and it looks good, then you have no problem. No matter what you uploaded, Createspace will have converted it to PDF and every time your book is printed, it is that PDF that will be used, not your originally uploaded word processor file.

EMBEDDING FONTS IN PDFS

PDF stands for Portable Document Format. The idea is that you define your document on your computer and whomever you pass it to, whether someone reading it on an iPad, or a printer such as Createspace, will see your PDF document exactly as you see it on your computer; it is *portable*.

Well, that's the theory. It's not quite as simple as that, and the biggest problem you are likely to face if you choose to upload a PDF format of your manuscript to Createspace (or Lulu) regards *embedding fonts*.

With font embedding you are guarding against the risk that the recipient of your PDF doesn't have the same fonts that you used to generate your file. So you include the font definitions *inside* the file, just to be sure. Sounds simple enough but it isn't reliable. Font-embedding problems are common, and this is a wider problem than Createspace or print on demand. Take a quick tour of the Createspace community forums and you will find many Createspace authors complaining about font embedding problems.

If you upload to Createspace Interior Reviewer and it complains about font-embedding issues, you have a real problem. Font definitions and PDF coding are complex, and unless you have PDF editing software, such as Adobe Acrobat (not the free reader, the version of Acrobat you have to pay for) there's not a lot you can do to look inside the PDF and change it.

Don't give up just yet. There are some things you can try, though, that might let you wriggle out of this problem.

- **Ignore the warning.** Carefully read the words of the message from Createspace. It might say something like: 'We found a problem with font-embedding, but fixed it for you. Check it looks all right.' In that situation, you can try some of the other suggestions below, but if they don't work, you might want to go ahead anyway. After all, you will get to eyeball the book proof. If that's not right, you can do something about it.

- **Change the way you create your PDF.** Try turning on the options for **Optimize for Standard** and **Options... | ISO 19005-1 Compliant (PDF/A)**

- **Don't upload a PDF. Try uploading a doc or docx or rtf.** Try all formats in case one works. In Word 2007+, make sure you are embedding font information as follows: **Office Button (the round button top-left) | Word Options | Save | Embed fonts in the file.**

- **Use a different application to generate your PDF.** For the ultimate in PDF control, you need Adobe Acrobat. There is a lot of help on the Createspace Community for Acrobat. The free Acrobat Reader isn't enough. The base-level Acrobat product that can edit PDF files is Adobe Acrobat Standard, which costs $300.

- **Check whether you really need all those fonts.** If you open up your PDF document inside the free Adobe Acrobat Reader (almost certainly, what your computer uses automatically to display PDF documents) you can see what fonts are in use. Click **File | Properties... | Fonts** This shows you the fonts *actually* in use and whether they are successfully embedded or not. You might be surprised by what you see there. I often see manuscripts where clients have worked to standardize fonts with their text, but have ignored their white space (By white space I mean the gaps between words, at either end of the paragraphs, or empty lines). When you're printing from Word to your local printer, it doesn't matter what font this whitespace uses. But your PDF file doesn't know this and will retain this menagerie of exotic and unnecessary fonts.

- **How to find where fonts are used.** Word's Find and Replace dialog can handle this. Open it up and click **Format | Font... | then select your font.** Make sure you've left the **Find what: box** empty. This finds the next occurrence of the font you selected. To turn this off, click the **No Formatting** button on the bottom of the Find and Replace dialog.

- **Try other fonts.** If you can't get your preferred font to embed, replace it with another one. Keep uploading to Interior Reviewer until it no longer complains. Hopefully you've followed my advice about using styles, because changing fonts is easy if all you need to do is change the style definition.

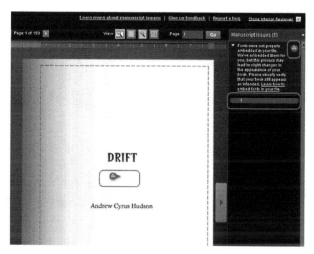

Figure 55: Font warnings in Createspace Interior Reviewer

Above is a screenshot of Createspace complaining about font embedding. When the Interior Reviewer gives warnings, you can click on the red warning triangle icon (at top-right) against each warning to bring up a list of pages where Interior Reviewer found that problem. In this case, I've only got one warning, and it's only found on page 1. I've clicked on the page number to open up that page. There's a red mark on the page, where Createspace is telling you where on the page it found the problem. In this example, the font with the embedding problem was only used for a blank line. It was a simple matter to replace with a different font and remove the warning.

FRONT MATTER

The front matter is all the stuff that goes at the front of your book before the main text starts. For print books, I would, as always, recommend taking a wide selection of books off your shelves and seeing what professional publishers do before reading further. For eBooks, I wouldn't go looking at eBooks from traditional publishing houses, as many of them produced poorly formatted eBooks until recently.

For formatting page numbers and headers in front matter, see [p94].

What to put in your front matter

Copyright, title, preface, logo of your publishing imprint, introduction, acknowledgement, dedication, and foreword (and make sure you write 'foreword', and not 'forward', though you would be in good company if you make that mistake).

If you aren't sure of whether you need to include any item on that list, then you probably don't need it. Err on the side of leaving out. For example, do you really need to print enormous lists of legalese, that you don't fully understand, in the hope that it will somehow prevent people from stealing your book? Just an 'All rights reserved' plus a copyright assertion covers it.

The minimum you need is:

- Title of book + author name

- Copyright page with copyright assertion (e.g. 'Copyright © Tim C. Taylor, 2013'), and ISBN number (ISBN is mandatory for Lulu).

That's the bare minimum, but I would pay the extra time and cost of a slightly more elaborate front matter, for the print book, otherwise your book can look overly frugal.

Here's a page-by-page breakdown of the front matter I will typically assemble for my Greyhart Press imprint:

1. Page 1 (facing) **Half Title Page** — Just the title, not the author name or anything else. Just this once, abandon the habit of using styles

for everything, and make it look as good as it can with whatever font looks best.

2. Page 2 (non-facing) **'Also by'** page — List books by the same author: Start with 'Also available by A. N. Author in Greyhart Press' at about 1/4 way down the page. Then, after a blank line, list other titles. Center all of this. If there aren't any other books, leave this page completely blank.

3. Page 3 (facing) **Title Page** — Repeat the title from the first page (possibly at reduced size but do use the same font). Give the author name (use a different font/weighting to the title). It is up to you whether you put your title or author name first. At the bottom, I put a centered Greyhart Press logo. If you have an imprint name, use it here. Some people insist that professional book layouts always give the author name *without* preceding with a 'by' (in other words 'Tim C. Taylor' rather than 'by Tim C. Taylor'). This isn't true, although it *is* more common to leave out the 'by'. With Greyhart Press books, I always give author name *without* the 'by' because that book might end up with a reviewer who mistakenly believes that is a sign of professionalism.

4. Page 4 (non-facing) **Copyright page** — Center the text here. The minimum you need is 'Copyright © Tim C. Taylor, 2013' and (for Lulu distribution) the ISBN number, though I would include the ISBN number for Createspace too. Try to keep to a single page and reduce the font size to fit it all in. If you have a lot to put in, consider separating blocks of text with blank spaces. If you are publishing a collection or anthology, list the original copyright dates and publication where each story was first published. If you want to say a few words of thanks, for example to the critique group who work-shopped your manuscript, put this at the bottom of the copyright page.

5. Page 5 (facing) **Dedication page** — Put the dedication between quarter and halfway down page and usually centered. As a variation, put a quotation here (in quotes and italics) and put the dedication at the top of the 'Also by page' (page 2).

6. Page 6 (non-facing) **Leave blank.**

7. Page 7 (facing) **Start the main part of your book here.** For novels, start with the Prologue, Chapter 1, or the title page for Part 1, as appropriate (and start counting page numbers at '1'). For non-fiction and collections/ anthologies, put the table of contents here.

Lulu's distribution agreements ask you to place a title page at the front, followed by a copyright page. A strict interpretation might suggest my Greyhart Press approach to front matter is Lulu-illegal. I've used this with Lulu, though, and experienced no problems.

Front matter for eBooks

The reading experience is different with eBooks. First of all, the screen size is smaller, which means your copyright page that crams a lot of information into a single page in the paperback edition might be four pages or more on an iPhone, especially if the fonts render larger than you hoped. This quickly becomes annoying. Secondly, font embedding is simply not consistent across devices. Lastly, and some would say of most importance, most eBooks are purchased from online retailer sites that allow some form of sample download, for example of the first 10%. The result is that for very short books (and certainly short stories) the sample doesn't reach very far into the story, not enough to hook the reader. For these reasons, some publishers put as much of the front matter as possible at the *back* of the book.

Here are some recommendations for eBook front matter:

- Don't use any blank pages. Or, at most, one between the end of the front matter and the start of the book.

- Use modest fonts for the title and author. I stick to maximum of 18 points, 180%, 1.8em (14pt, 140%, 1.4em for Smashwords) and use common fonts, not elaborate ones.

- Don't have a separate title page; go straight to the title/ author/ imprint page.

- Smashwords has specific requirements for title and copyright assertion. They are listed in the *Smashwords Style Guide*.

- If your book needs a table of contents, and you think that it helps people browsing the front of your book to decide they want to buy, then keep it at the front. For example, a reference book or an anthology of stories by different authors might sell if browsers look at the table of contents and see topics or authors they want to read. In other cases, consider putting the table of contents at the end, even though this contravenes Amazon's recommendations for Kindle books.

- Trim the copyright page content as much as possible.

- If you have a print edition, make sure you *do not* use the same ISBN number for your eBook. However, it is a good idea to say something like 'also available in paperback, ISBN xxx-xxx-xxx'. The ISBN is unique to each edition of your book. If you have hardback, paperback, Kindle format, EPUB format, and Smashwords edition, and you want an ISBN for each, then you need five separate ISBNs (though, personally, I rarely bother with an ISBN for Kindle-format books).

ADDING BLANK PAGES AT THE END OF THE BOOK

With Createspace, there is no need to add additional pages at the end of the book. It used to be with Lulu that you needed to ensure that your book had a number of pages exactly divisible by four. Createspace will add those extra pages for you automatically if it needs them. Lulu currently asks for at least one blank page at the end of the book.

You will have to pay for these pages.

The reason for this strange divide-by-four rule is that some printers will print four (or eight) book pages onto one large sheet of paper.

On the other hand, I sometimes add a half dozen spare pages at the end of the book as a buffer to fill any additional page requirements that might arise for future revisions due to errata, additional text, or new cross-selling back matter. The purpose is to avoid situations where I have to resize and and re-upload the cover because the additional pages have nudged the spine into needing resizing.

WIDOWS AND ORPHANS

These are typesetting concepts. The Wikipedia entry starts as follows:

*In typesetting, **widows** and **orphans** are words or short lines at the beginning or end of a paragraph, which are left dangling at the top or bottom of a column, separated from the rest of the paragraph. There is some disagreement about the definitions of widow and orphan; what one source calls a widow the other calls an orphan.*

All you need to know in Word is that:

- When a paragraph is split across two pages, it can look untidy.

- To fix this, all you need do is set the **Paragraph**s in your style definitions so the **Widow/ Orphan control** is turned on. Let Word do the rest.

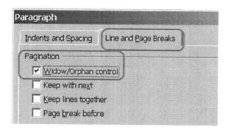

Figure 56: Widow/ Orphan control

I've never had a problem with Word's Widow/orphan control. Professional typesetters sometimes scoff that what Word does automatically is not as good as a professional typesetter. I'm sure they are right, but I doubt your readers would notice the difference.

I would stay well clear of formatting widow/ orphan control by hand because:

- Handcrafted widow controls are locked. If you subsequently revise your text, or publish at a different page size, you will invalidate the formatting because page breaks will no longer occur at the same place; it could look awful.

- With eBooks you *cannot ever assume where the page breaks will fall*. If you handcraft the widow control, or anything to do with justification or pagination, the results will look truly awful. *Guaranteed.*

TABLE OF CONTENTS

For anthologies and most non-fiction, a table of contents (TOC) is essential for readers to find their way around your book. It's also a way of showing off the contents of your book for potential browsers, and that includes the 'Look Inside' image of your Createspace book that Amazon will put onto your book's page on Amazon.

Other than anthologies and compilations, most fiction does not benefit from a TOC.

For most purposes, Microsoft's tool for generating tables of contents automatically does a good job and is probably more flexible than you realize. It's what I used for the print edition of the book you're reading now.

The beauty of inserting an automatic table of contents (from the Ribbon, pick REFERENCES | TABLE OF CONTENTS) is that Word does all the hard work of finding all your headings, automatically adding them into your TOC, and correctly adding your page numbers. If your book changes, you can tell your TOC to update itself and all the page numbers and headings will recalculate themselves. You can update the TOC in several ways: the simplest is from the Ribbon, REFERENCES | TABLE OF CONTENTS | UPDATE TABLE.

Microsoft's online help for the topic of tables of contents is extensive. One of the best places to start is with Microsoft's Word 2013 training videos on this subject. I'm not aware of any changes to tables of contents since Word 2007, so the 2013 video should apply at least as far back as 2007. These training courses use Microsoft Powerpoint .pptx format. If you can't read that straight away, you can download a free viewer from Microsoft or try running it using Quicktime.

The course I have in mind is called "Advanced tables of contents". You can Google for it, or go to http://office.microsoft.com/en-gb/word-help/advanced-tables-of-contents-RZ104046874.aspx

---

The key to Microsoft's automatic TOC is your use of styles. By default, Word will look through your text and pick out your heading styles (for example, 'heading1', 'heading2') and use those as TOC entries.

Once you've created a TOC, you will be able to modify TOC STYLES in the Styles Pane. The first level TOC entries are styled by the TOC1 style. The next level by a style called TOC2, and so on.

The heading of the TOC has its own style called TOC Heading.

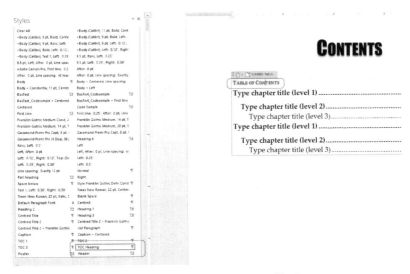

Figure 57: Using styles to drive the automatic table of contents

Look up similar books to yours in the library or your bookshelf to get ideas on styling to aim for. Also, make good use of the Look Inside feature on Amazon, though make sure you are looking at the print edition.

As well as the automatic table of contents, Word allows a Custom TOC from the same part of the Ribbon. This allows you to fine-tune the design, and to fill the TOC using other styles than heading styles.

There's plenty of further guidance on this topic online. If you need such sophistication as multiple TOCs, sub-headings and summaries, then Word can do this if you learn a few field codes.

Alternatively, if you need flexibility, it could be easiest to abandon Microsoft's TOC generator altogether and write and style the TOC yourself, something I've done myself for several poetry and short story anthologies.

I've reproduced below a table of contents I made for *Dead to Rights: A Circularity of Glosas*, a poetry anthology by Alain C. Dexter. Typing in the entries and styling the TOC yourself is easy, but to type in the page numbers by hand is dangerous. It would be so easy to get them wrong, especially if the correct page numbers change after editing.

3. North: Wisdom

4. East: Higher Ground

5. Center: Mastery

The trick is to use CROSS-REFERENCES, which you can access from the Ribbon under REFERENCES | CAPTIONS | CROSS-REFERENCE. For our purposes, we want reference type: *Heading* and insert reference to: *Page number,* as with the screenshot below.

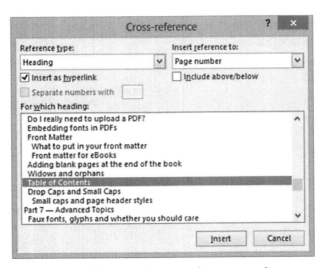

Figure 58: Using cross-references to reference page numbers

When you hit the Insert button, the correct page number appears in the TOC. If the page number changes at a later date, the cross-reference doesn't change automatically to match (which is the same as Word's automatic TOC). To make sure all the page numbers are accurate, do this:

- **Save your document**
- **Select the entire contents of your document** (CTRL+A if you're running Windows, ⌘ + A if on a Mac)
- **Update field codes** (F9. If you're running a Mac and that doesn't update field codes, you must first turn off the Exposé keyboard shortcut for this key. On the Apple menu, click System Preferences. Under Personal, click Exposé & Spaces)

In the print edition of the book you are reading, you will see entries such as *For more information on cross-references, see [p218].*

Those page numbers are cross-references and use the technique I've just explained. Where I want to refer to a specific page rather than a heading, I insert a bookmark (Ribbon: INSERT I Links I Bookmark) and then in the cross-reference dialog I pick Bookmark as the reference type.

If you're writing non-fiction then cross-references can be a powerful tool. If you've not used them before, open up a new document in Word and start playing with them. I've just run through a lot of dialogs and key presses, but once you've used them a few times, you'll find them easy, I promise!

A final word about your TOC. Word TOCs use tabs and page numbers. Neither have any place in eBooks. Never allow an automatic tool to convert your paperback table of contents directly into your eBook as it will look awful.

The table of contents customization allows you to set table of contents entries as hyperlinks. Depending on how you create your eBook, this might be all you need to set the hyperlinks that your eBook TOC must have in place of page numbers.

DROP CAPS AND SMALL CAPS

Drop caps are another way of making the first page of a chapter stand out. Look, here's a drop cap now...

Figure 59: Drop Caps

A two-line drop cap (such as my example) is fairly common in modern fiction. An unscientific sampling of books on my shelves reveals about half of my books have some combination of drop cap and/ or the small caps that I'll show you in a moment. The genre of the book doesn't make much difference. To insert drop caps in Word 2007-13, use the Drop Cap button on the insert menu (see screen above). For Word 2003, click on the paragraph and then **Format | Drop Cap | Dropped**

Instead of, or as well as, the drop cap, some book layouts have small caps for the first few words, or perhaps the entire first line (see next screenshot for an example). I like to set small caps for the first four words. I don't take any account of how long those words are — just the first four.

To use small caps, select the text, and then format the font to use that effect (see second screenshot below). Since I use small caps frequently, I've used Word's customize feature to add a small caps button into the Ribbon.

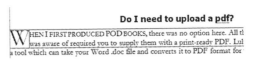

Figure 60: Drop Cap + Small Caps

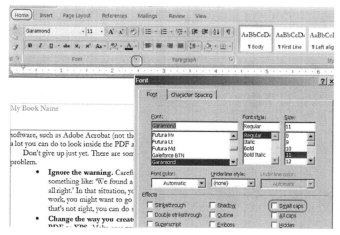

Figure 61: Setting Small Caps in Word

With extreme caution, you might want to explore implementing drop caps using images. You can easily get carried away here and make your formatting too fussy. If your formatting distracts from the story in a fiction book, then it's poor formatting. But for some children's books or some genres, such as high fantasy, you might want to explore something like this...

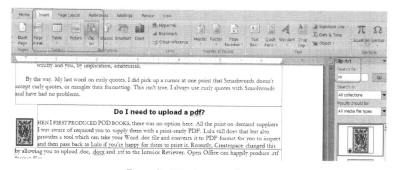

Figure 62: Using images as drop caps

Office Online provides clip art that you can use as drop caps. Select **Insert | Clip Art** and in the **Search for** box, simply type the letter you want. Then click on the image of the letter, resize it (or better still, save it locally and resize it in another application — although Office clip art is often something called vector graphics, which means it usually resizes okay by dragging the corner handles of the image). Making sure you've clicked on your image, from the Ribbon, select **Picture Tools | Format | Text Wrapping | Square**.

Small caps and page header styles

Another common use of small caps is for page headers, where it's a useful way of keeping the header text distinct from the body text without drawing attention to it.

There are other uses of small caps in the body of your book that all boil down making some text stand out as distinct. The only reason to do this, never let us forget, is to make your book easier to read.

Example of this might be:

- Army and corps names in your book about the Napoleonic Wars
- Album names in your non-fiction book about the music industry of the 1970s — you might put albums in small caps and song titles in italics.
- In your fantasy novels about the Goblin Wars, you might show goblin dialogue in small caps to distinguish from human speech.

Part 7 — Advanced Topics

Typography 101 • OpenType special effects • Kerning • Typography 909 • Faux fonts & style-linking • How to republish your back catalog • Cover art tips • More on margins • Createspace vs. Lulu & LSI • Advanced color spaces, dot gain & PDF settings • Going beyond Microsoft Word • Text boxes and WordArt • Where to find further information

TYPOGRAPHY 101

We're going to be talking about fonts. Before we do, it makes sense to introduce a few basic terms and concepts in TYPOGRAPHY: the science and art of lettering. Let's look at a letter

A

Don't worry, I'm not going all Sesame Street on you. 'A' is the only letter we need. We're interested in typography here, so let me describe that specific letter 'A' as it appears in the paperback version of this book.

That character is an upper case letter 'A' which is part of a FONT called *Times New Roman*. Instead of a 'character' I might also refer to it as a GLYPH, which means one entry in the list of characters and other shapes defined in the font. We'll see more about glyphs in a moment.

Now let's look at another glyph.

A

It's still an 'A' and if I'm running Microsoft Word under Windows, then my Font menu in the Ribbon still says it is Times New Roman. However, the definition of the glyph actually comes from a *different* font file. This time it comes from the *Times New Roman Italic* font file, a font where the glyph for every letter slants to the right.

The fact that Windows does all this in the background for you is usually a good thing. All you need to know is that the 'I' button makes text italic and 'B' makes it bold. Not only that, but with most fonts – certainly almost all those that come with Windows and Microsoft Office, the result will be a true italic or bold glyph and not a glyph that has been created on the fly and can look ugly (what's called a *faux glyph*). If you're very unlucky though, this can go wrong as I'll explain shortly in *Typography 909*.

Mac OS works differently from Windows: all the font variants in the font family are presented in font dialogs. You get to see Times New Roman Italic listed as a separate font from Times New Roman, and you get to see Times New Roman Bold, and Bold Italic too.

Under the hood, Macs work the same way as Windows in that if you select some text in Times New Roman font and press the 'I' button to make it italic – then this will automatically change the font for that text to Times New Roman Italic. Macs allow the additional option of selecting text and then changing the font of that text to be an italic or bold font, or whatever.

Some handy definitions

People mix up terms such as 'typeface' and 'fonts'. It can get confusing so I've set out below the definitions that I use.

Font — a set of characters (called glyphs). For example, Times New Roman Bold, Times New Roman, and Times New Roman Italic are each separate fonts.

Typeface — a set of related fonts. For example, Times New Roman is a typeface that consists for a normally weighted font, a bold font, an italic font, and a bold-italic font.

'Typeface family' — Some typefaces have 'sibling' fonts. For example, Deja Vu family has monospace, sans-serif, and serif typefaces. In practice, the difference between typeface and typeface family isn't always so clear cut. When picking fonts to use, selecting fonts from the same typeface family is one good approach because the fonts will not 'fight' each other. Typeface family is not a widely used term, but the concept is worth knowing.

Faux glyphs — where Word knows you want a character to be bold, small cap or whatever, but builds the glyph for you by altering the regular glyph rather than picking a font that is designed to be bold, or small cap etc.

Special Effects with OpenType

If you look up the fonts on your computer you will see nearly all are defined as TrueType or OpenType (in Windows you do this from the Fonts section of the

Control Panel app). OpenType For our purposes the difference between the two formats is that OpenType allows font designers standard ways to define fancy variations such as LIGATURES, STYLISTIC SETS, and NUMBER STYLES. Because they are defined in a standard way, Word 2010 and later can let you use them directly from the Ribbon.

Other than that, the differences between TrueType and OpenType are unimportant with one exception: older versions of Windows may crash when using certain OpenType fonts in Word (those that use something called 'Postscript outlines'). Certainly I found OpenType fonts unstable when I was briefly running Word 2010 on Windows XP. I am typing these words in Word 2013 on Windows 8 where OpenType and TrueType both work equally well.

To access these OpenType features you need Word 2010 or later. From the font dialog you're familiar with, move to the Advanced tab. Word 2013 makes these easier to get to. From the Ribbon click the text effects button from the Font section of the Home menu. Underneath the text effects such as shadow and outline, you get access to the OpenType features.

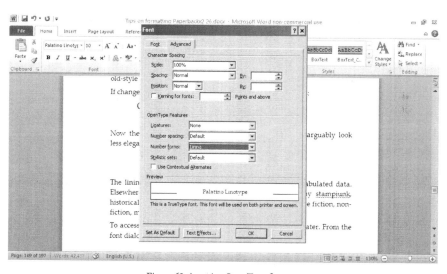

Figure 63 Accessing OpenType features

Ligatures

Ligatures are combinations of characters that are bound together into a single glyph, such as combining 'f' and 'l' into a single glyph fl. They can add a little flash if you want old-fashioned ornate titles, but are rarely used. To use them, pick a Ligature option other than 'none' and Word will automatically substitute a ligature for predefined character combinations.

The ligature that got away.

There is one ligature that is so popular, we no longer know that's what it is. The Latin word 'et' means 'and'. The et ligature was in common everyday use in Roman times and never went away. Today we call it the ampersand.

Number forms

Number forms are more important because they can cause problems if you don't realize what they are.

Take these example chapter titles. I'm using Constantia font with default settings.

Chapter 76

The weight of the '7' and '6' is centered consistently and by design, but some people will look at that and think the '7' is in the wrong place. Where I've used this number form in novels, I've had plenty of beta readers complain that the '7' is somehow in a subscript setting and that this is an error. It's not. It's how the 'old-style' NUMBER FORM is defined for this and several other fonts. In the case of Constantia, old-style is the default number form.

If change the number form from 'default' to 'lining', I get this:

Chapter 76

Now the numbers are vertically aligned at their tops but arguably look less elegant.

Old-style: 0123456789

Lining: 0123456789

The lining number form is easier to read if you're using tabulated data. Elsewhere it's a matter of taste. I'd use old-style for my steampunk, historical adventure, romance novel and lining for my science fiction, non-fiction, or modern-day spy thriller.

Stylistic sets

Font designers can design variations of their fonts with some or all characters. There aren't many fonts that use this feature. Gabriola from Microsoft is one that does.

Recent versions of the *Impact* font provided by Microsoft as part of Windows also have stylistic sets, as you can see in this postcard I produced to advertise my Greyhart Press business locally.

Figure 64: Advanced OpenType features in practice

The special way the letters 'E' and 'R' combine and 'T' and 'H' are also contextual alternatives. Or at least, that's how I think of them. In actual fact, in Word, the contextual alternative box makes no difference for the Impact font; you get the fancy alternatives by picking stylistic sets instead. And yet how each word is styled depends on the letters contain within it.

I think it's best to consider the distinction loose, dependent on the font designer's interpretation, and just have fun and play. While playing, though, remember that a little 'flash' goes a long way in typography. In my postcard example, I wanted to get across the message that a local publisher from a small town in England, had topped the bestseller charts across the Atlantic in America. That's why I only used the fancy stylistic sets in the three places that most got that message across, while keeping the other text plain.

AND ALL THAT IS AVAILABLE IN WORD.
FROM THIS IMPACT to THAT and THAT

Contextual Alternatives

If you tick this box, then the font design can override certain combinations of characters. It is very font-specific and not very common, but an example would be a cursive script (one that looks like handwriting) that replaces certain common words ('of' 'and' 'the') with contextual alternative glyphs designed specifically for use with those words. Put another way, the font might tell Word that instead of using the normal glyphs for the letters 'a', 'n', and 'd', it should use special glyphs designed specifically to produce an especially neat version of 'and'.

Kerning & Spacing

If you look back at the advanced font tab, there's an entry there for Kerning. This isn't specific to OpenType fonts and is something you should keep an eye on with your titles. Kerning refers to moving characters closer together to avoid unnecessary gaps. It's generally a good thing to have kerning set on for headings and titles. For example if you have a capital W followed by a lower case 'a', where should the 'a' start? With kerned text the 'a' will shelter somewhat under the 'W', which looks neater and more professional. With Word up to and including Word 2013, there is no control to fine tune kerning: it is either on or off.

Wa — without kerning

Wa — with kerning

Back in the advanced font tab, you will see a SPACING option. This simply places a gap between characters if EXPANDED or reduces spacing if CONDENSED. Best used for special effects and titles, I've given expanded examples below for an idea of how chapter headings might look. I've set the first example to have normal spacing, then expanded 3 points, and then expanded 9 points.

CHAPTER UNSPACED

CHAPTER SPACED

S P A C E D   T O O

You can also have different settings for each character within the same paragraph. For example:

CHAPTER 13
D E A T H   O R   G L O R Y

Here I've added a manual line feed between the two lines (Shift + Enter). The first line has normal spacing and the second 6pt expanded, except for the final letter ('Y') which has normal spacing (because otherwise the subtitle would be offset from the right-hand margin).

Of course, you could achieve an expanded effect by adding space characters, but if you're doing this frequently (e.g. with chapter headings) then it is easier and more consistent to apply and change if you are setting expanded characters through a heading style rather than direct formatting.

We've done the introductions and the fun stuff. Now we'll look in more detail at fonts to dispel rumors and solve potential problems concerning:

- Faux fonts
- Small caps revisited
- How to check your font capability
- Font style-linking and pitfalls in transferring Word files from Mac to Windows

Faux Fonts

A *faux* font is one that is faked. So faux bold text, for example, would be the normal weighted typeface but crudely fattened up. With a slightly more sophisticated typeface, there will be a version of the font that is specifically designed to be bold. There will be another that is specifically designed to be italic, another for small caps, and possibly even more variations designed to be used at different sizes. The basic fonts you will be familiar with (such as Garamond, Times New Roman, Arial, Verdana, Tahoma) all have proper bold and italic fonts, so you are in no danger of faux fonts there.

Are faux fonts really such an evil? It depends on the typefaces. These days all common typefaces I'm aware of come with italic and bold versions, and all of them have something called font style-linking (which means that Word knows that when you tell it to set text in italics, for example, that it has to go pick the glyphs from the italic font). So the typefaces that don't do all this for you are obscure, amateur or specialist —designed to perform a specific task. So, yes, if you force a typeface to use faux fonts, it probably means you're forcing it to do something it's not designed for, and that will look bad.

So now that we've understood that faux fonts are ones that have been made by altering the normal font, rather than being designed specifically for that purpose, we come to faux small caps.

With small caps, Word lets us down. It's easy enough to set text to use Small Caps (from the font dialog that we've seen before) but these are faux glyphs Even if you have fonts that contain small cap glyphs, Microsoft can't access them …

... at least, not easily. If you are desperate for genuine small caps, you can insert them from INSERT | SYMBOL if they exist in the font. If they are there then they will most likely appear in the section called 'Private Use Area'. Inserting characters one by one is not my idea of a good time, but is perfectly practical for a heading or part title, for example.

Also, a few typefaces have a specific font for small caps, such as Fontin. To switch to small caps, select the text and change font from 'Fontin' to 'Fontin Smallcaps'.

So what is all the fuss? Below I've written out text in real and faux small caps using a paid-for font called Adobe Garamond Pro.

SMALL CAPS (*real*), SMALL CAPS (*faux*) & SMALL CAPS (*faux –with reduced font size*)

The lower case letters come out much larger with the faux small caps, so to the right I've reduced their font size by a point to match the real small caps on the left. There certainly is a difference even then. The strokes are narrower; in fact, at these fairly small point sizes (10pt with the faux small caps reduced to 9pt), it isn't easy to read.

If I raise the font size to 11pt (10pt for the reduced small caps) then we get...

SMALL CAPS (*real*), SMALL CAPS (*faux*) & SMALL CAPS (*faux –reduced*)

All of them are easy to read, the default Word small caps is too 'shouty' for my tastes, especially when mixed in with normal text (rather than used in titles and headings), and reducing the font size of the faux small caps makes the strokes look weedy. All of this, of course, applies to just one typeface.

So the issue of faux small caps is not something that exists only in the minds of overly conservative typographers, but whether that means you should never use them is something else entirely. My view is that you should be guided by your eye. If it looks good and is clear then use them. I use faux small caps extensively in the paperback version of this book because I feel the end result is clearer for you to read than not using them. When I do use real small caps it is normally for title pages.

How to tell what your font can do

So you've picked your favorite fonts for your book. Does it have bold and italic glyphs or are they faked? With Macs, this is easy because, like or not, each individual typeface in the font family is listed in font picking controls. With Windows, you need to go to Control Panel | Fonts to see what's going on.

Here's a shot from Windows XP showing some of my fonts.

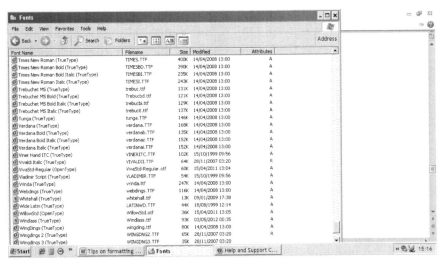

Figure 65: Explore your fonts in Windows XP

At the top we have our old favorite, Times New Roman, and, yes, it comes in regular, bold, bold italic, and italic flavors. There are no faux glyphs here (except for small caps). Trebuchet and Verdana have the full set too, but some of the less familiar fonts do not. Take *Viner Hand ITC* for example. *This is a 'script' font that looks like joined-up handwriting. Like most script fonts, there is no italic and no bold available.* Think about it for a moment, real handwriting doesn't have any concept of bold or italics; you would use underline instead.

So if I tell Word to set some Viner Hand ITC in bold italic, then it will have to fake it. And if that doesn't look good it's because we're trying to do something the font was not designed for and not a fault of International Typeface Corporation (ITC: The initials you sometimes see after a font name represent the organization who designed the font).

The equivalent dialog in Windows 8 makes this a little clearer.

Figure 66 Explore your fonts in Windows 8

Many of the fonts that only come in one flavor are display fonts designed for titles or other small blocks of text.

Some people talk of faux styling as an unspeakable evil. Frankly I think in most cases it's a minor detail worth getting right if you're a perfectionist, but most people reading your book wouldn't recognize a faux bold in a million years, and if you pointed it out wouldn't care. *In most cases.* THERE ARE EXCEPTIONS! And the most common come with fancy display fonts that you would never use in body text such as this one: *Sinking Ship,* designed by Corianton Hale.

It can look wonderful for a:

BOOK TITLE,

BOOK COVER,

CHAPTER TITLE

BUT TRY USING THE FONT IN YOUR BODY TEXT, A PURPOSE IT WAS NEVER DESIGNED FOR, AND AFTER TWENTY PAGES OR SO YOUR READERS WILL SUE YOU FOR GIVING THEM A MIGRAINE.

Sinking Ship comes as a regular typeface only. In the next image, I've repeated the same text in regular, faux bold, and faux bold italic. The bold is blockier, loses the grunge effect inside the characters, and increases the amount of noise. It's not as good, but not as disastrous as some fonts in faux bold. The faux bold italic, though, does look awful. The sloping lines are heavily pixelated (it has the 'jaggies') and some characters, particularly the 'A' just look plain wrong. I'm not talking the designer untidiness of a well-designed grunge font, it looks to me like an eight year old with a leaking heavy duty marker pen has tried to write in a Star Trek font but hasn't got it quite right yet.

CHAPTER TITLE
CHAPTER TITLE
CHAPTER TITLE

Font style-linking

I mentioned in Typography 101 that whether on Windows or Mac OS, Word knows that when you set text to italic using CTRL+I (or defining the style to use italic or pressing the 'I' button) that it automagically knows to go pick the glyphs from the italic font rather than the regular font. This is called FONT STYLE-LINKING and the rules for font style-linking are defined inside each font. The font files are defined to an open standard and so the same rules for font style-linking apply the same on Macs and Windows.

If you stick to the fonts provided by Microsoft and stick to either a Mac or to Windows, then you will never have a problem.

I've written this topic to provide you with a little more understanding of style-linking just in case you do encounter a problem.

Problems are likely to be one of these scenarios:

1. Transfer a Word document from Mac to Windows. Text is set in italics through picking an italic font. Windows Word shows the right font but doesn't understand that it's meant to be styled as italic. This isn't normally a problem unless you do something like tell the Find dialog to find italic text (which, unfortunately for me is what I do every time I build an eBook from Word).

2. A non-Microsoft typeface does not have style-linking (or none that Word understands). So, even though you have (for example) a normal font and a bold font, if you press Ctrl+B to style text as bold, Word doesn't understand how to pick the bold font. Instead, Word creates a faux bold glyph by fattening up the normally weighted glyph.

Adobe is a major producer of fonts. To get an idea of how this style-linking works, and how fonts might be listed differently on Mac and Windows, take a look at their PDF document listing Adobe fonts and mapping Mac to Windows.
http://store.adobe.com/type/pdfs/Type1-2-OpenType.pdf

I've listed a typeface called Adobe Caslon Pro as an example. From the section of Adobe's document, the middle column is the font list you would see surfaced in an OS X application, such as Word 2011 for Mac. The right-hand column shows the fonts + style information for Windows. With Adobe Caslon Pro, there are too many fonts in the family to fit into one 'font slot' in Windows. So, instead, you see two fonts listed in Windows: Adobe Caslon Pro, and Adobe Caslon Pro Bold.

Caslon Pro typeface on Mac and Windows

This is the name of the font	The name you pick from the list of fonts on a Mac	The name you pick from the list of fonts in Windows, plus any additional styling required
Adobe Caslon Pro-Bold	Adobe Caslon Pro Bold	Adobe Caslon Pro Bold
Adobe Caslon Pro-BoldItalic	Adobe Caslon Pro Bold Italic	Adobe Caslon Pro Bold + italic style
Adobe Caslon Pro-Italic	Adobe Caslon Pro Italic	Adobe Caslon Pro + italic style
Adobe Caslon Pro-Regular	Adobe Caslon Pro	Adobe Caslon Pro
Adobe Caslon Pro-Semibold	Adobe Caslon Pro SmBd	Adobe Caslon Pro + bold style
Adobe Caslon Pro-SemiboldItalic	Adobe Caslon Pro SmBd Italic	Adobe Caslon Pro + bold & italic styles

Figure 67: Mapping fonts to Mac and Windows

To see what that looks like in Windows, I've taken screen shots of

- The font section of the Control Panel in Windows 8 (which lists the font files)
- The font selection list box in Word 2013 (showing the only two Caslon Pro fonts displayed here)
- The font selection controls in Adobe Photoshop CS6 (Windows)

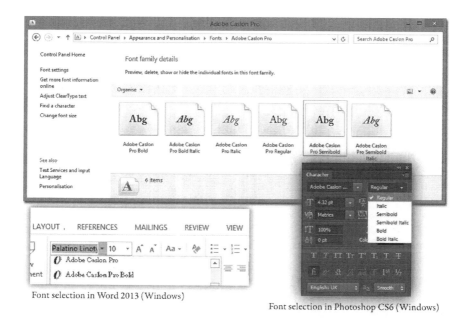

Font selection in Word 2013 (Windows)

Font selection in Photoshop CS6 (Windows)

Figure 68: Adobe Caslon Pro font in Windows

I've heard of Mac users seeing Windows and despairing that all the fonts have disappeared. They haven't. But for typefaces with a lot of fonts, it isn't always obvious how to pick the desired font.

For example, here's how you pick Adobe Caslon Pro Semibold from the font menu in Word

Word for Mac: pick *Adobe Caslon Pro Semibold* from the font selection list.

Word for Windows: pick *Adobe Caslon Pro* from the font selection list and then style it bold.

I think Mac users have a point!

And if you thought Caslon Pro was awkward yet manageable, consider Adobe Garamond Premier Pro. This is an Adobe Opticals font which means that not only does it have different sets of glyphs for bold and semibold etc, but it also has different designs for different sizes. So there's a whole set of CAPTION fonts for really small sizes, SUBHEAD for smaller headings and DISPLAY for large headings and display uses such as posters. In total there are 34 fonts in the family, of which 13 are surfaced as separate fonts in the Windows font picker, which is pretty confusing.

In the screenshot below, I've shown the fonts surfaced in Adobe Photoshop. All of them together make up just one typeface.

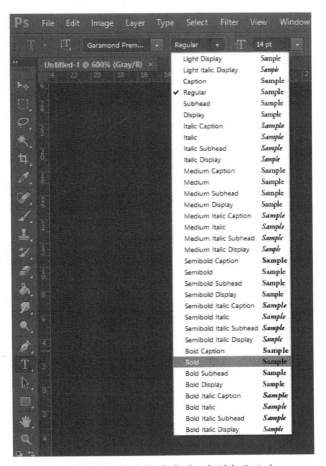

Figure 69: Fonts by the bucketload with Adobe Opticals

Finally, while I've just talked about font style-linking, there are a few fonts I'm aware of where these links are *not* defined. I recently acquired a font as a subscriber reward from Adobe. It's called Leander Script. The release notes state clearly that there is a bold and a regular variant but there is no font style-linking. Setting bold by styling the regular font generates a faux bold glyph.

Leander script looks really good — it certainly isn't missing font style-linking as a result of being made on the cheap — but I suspect it has been designed by an organization that does not use Windows computers.

Such fonts are rare, but if you go exploring for new fonts, you will find other examples, so take care!

That's plenty enough about fonts for this book. If you're interested in the topic, there is a wealth of information available online, including many examples of fine typography by experts in the art. Here are some sites I recommend:

http://www.thebookdesigner.com

http://typophile.com/blog

http://www.typographyserved.com

HOW TO REPUBLISH YOUR BACK CATALOG

I've worked with a number of authors who have a back catalog of traditionally printed books for which the rights have now reverted to them. This throws up a number of problems.

If you have your original Word or other word processing document, then your task is much easier, but take care with copy editing. Most commonly the document file you have is what was sent to the publisher *before* final copy editing. In other words, you need to go through copy editing again. Even if the bulk of copy editing is contained within your Word document, it's common for a few last minute changes to have been made at the publisher's end.

If your publisher gave you a PDF of the finished book, then this carries its own problems. You can convert a PDF to Word format, but the result is not pretty but still a better result than the last resort: scanning.

This is the most common way to re-publish an old book in my experience. Take a paperback, scan the pages using an OCR scanner (Optical Character Recognition), assemble the scans into a single Word document, tidy, format, republish.

This sounds simple, after all most inkjet printers can do OCR scanning these days, but scanning isn't as easy as it looks, and even the best scanning will leave many difficult-to-spot errors.

The first task is to turn the printed version of your book into a single Word document. The best way is to pay a professional to do this. Google for 'book scanning' services in your country and get some quotes. You're looking here for a service provided by a printing company. If you have the time and patience you can do this yourself with a cheap multi-function printer, but expect the professionals to do a faster and better job of it.

Even a professional job will still be loaded with errors. For example, suppose you have a character in your novel called 'Saul'. The OCR software will have a hard time telling the difference between 'Saul' and 'Soul'. Your spell checker will not complain about either. Most problems can be identified by reading out aloud or converting to an eBook format and getting your iPad or Kindle or whatever to read to you. But in the case of 'Saul' / 'Soul' even that won't help.

And a more amateurish job will be laden with spelling errors for you to address. The OCR software will struggle to differentiate between the number '1' and the lower-case character 'l'. '6' and 'b' may look the same depending on the font. It may decide an opening double quote is actually a superscript 'm' and a closing double quote is a superscript '3'.

The best approach is to accept that tidying a scanned book is a lengthy task. Use a variety of techniques at the start, and then expect to use beta readers to pick up the few examples you missed.

Here are some techniques to use:

- Distrust every use of a numeral. Check for every use of the number '1'. Then search for every use of '2' etc.
- Investigate every single spelling error reported by Word (usually shown with a red underline). If you are certain the word is correct but isn't in Word's dictionary, click the option to 'add to dictionary'.
- Investigate every grammar error (usually shown with a green underline). Yes, I know this is tedious. Word will report scores of grammar errors where you know better. Sometimes when there is an error in your manuscript, Word can't identify the error directly, but knows something isn't right and so flags a grammar error. In other words, when the grammar checker finds a genuine error the grammar rule it tells you has been broken is usually nonsense, but if you look deeper into the sentence, there is a real error lurking underneath. Remember the example above of 'Soul'/ 'Saul'? There is a good chance that the grammar checker will spot this.
- Investigate every suggested word. Word 2007 started putting blue squiggly lines under words it thinks you might have mistaken and suggests what you should have put. For example *it's* and *its*. With each new edition of Word this seems to get more accurate. You should be looking at these in any case, but if you're scanning in a book, go through all the blue squiggles now.
- Get a computer to read the results back. There are various ways to do this. The easiest is on an eReader such as Kindle or iPad/iPhone. Check your manual to see whether your device manages text-to-speech.
  - On your computer, download a free eBook management tool called Calibre.
  - Save your manuscript from Word as html format.
  - From Calibre, Add Book. Browse to the html file you saved and add that.
  - Convert the book to the required format. MOBI for Kindles and ePUB for everything else.

- Connect your device to your computer using your USB cable.
- Once Calibre has detected your device, right click the book on your Calibre library screen and 'send to main memory' on your device.
- From Calibre, eject your device.
- Disconnect your eReader and set your device's text-to-speech option running.
- Doing this with Apple tablets and phones doesn't always work. Apple wants you to do everything through iTunes. I use Dropbox to send myself files to my iPad, but you could email yourself.

COVER ART TIPS

This book is about formatting your *interior*. A few thoughts on covers, though:

- It's worth doing your book justice by getting an artist involved. That said, the Createspace and (the new) Lulu cover templates are fairly good, so long as your cover art image is good to start with.
- Assuming you want an eBook and a paperback, get the cover design done for both at the same time. For most people, the key image that determines whether your book will sell or not is how your front cover appears in a thumbnail on a computer or tablet screen. This is true for your eBook, but it is also true for your paperback. *Images that are only clear in paperback and do not look good in a thumbnail will cripple your sales.*
- Think about image resolution (dots per inch). If you create an eBook with the idea of following up later with a print edition, your artwork should reflect that now. The cover image for your print edition should be at least 300dpi. Suppose you want a 10 inch by 8 inch book; that means the cover image needs to be *at least 3000 pixels high (10 x 300 = 3000)*. Add in bleed and it's actually 3250.
- Until 2013, eBook covers were typically 600 x 800 pixels. That's no longer the case. Amazon, iBooks, and Smashwords have significantly upped the specification for their eBook covers. Essentially, they now want you to upload the front cover of your paperback with no reduction in the number of pixels (though they require sRGB colorspace and Amazon wants 72dpi).
- If your eBook cover is old (600 x 800 pixels) then that isn't going to be good enough to upload to your Createspace Cover Creator. You could enlarge the image and resample, but that will give a blurred image.
- Createspace provides a tool for calculating the dimensions you need to provide with your cover. Pay very close attention, and don't assume the guidance is the same as the last time you printed a book. Unfortunately, the size will probably be slightly different to the dimensions demanded by Lulu.
- Createspace recently got a lot tighter on spine art requirements for small books. The Cover Creator tool requires you to have at least 131 pages before it will allow you to add spine text. If you create your own cover, Createspace demands a blank spine for less than 100 pages. The implication for short books is that you might want to add extra margin

size, or larger font / leading, in order to bring your page count over 130 pages so that you can set spine text in the Cover Creator.

- Many very good and experienced paperback cover designers don't understand how to prepare books for Createspace. A lot of good artists don't understand how to design images for paperback books. A lot of traditional book cover artists are not very good at designing eBook covers and don't understand the vital importance of thumbnail images for paperbacks as well as eBooks.
- In summary, artists who have been creating book cover art for years don't always appreciate that the needs of self-publishers have seen rapid change in the past few years. Suddenly they are out of date. Here are some points to check with your artist. If you get the impression that they don't grasp these points or don't take you seriously, pass them by and try someone else.

Here's the list of points to check with your potential artist.

- o You want the same cover image for eBook and paperback front cover.
- o The eBook must be in sRGB colorspace and must have the same number of pixels as the front cover of the paperback book (remind them that the days of eBook covers being 600x800 pixels are now ancient history).
- o The front cover must look good in a thumbnail 400 pixels wide, and ideally 200 pixels wide. If it isn't then it's of no use. This is equally as true of your paperback as your eBook (unless you know you can sell paperbacks directly, perhaps as part of your consultancy business).
- o Paperback cover images (for any printer) must have a bleed and text needs to be set away from the trim edge and fold lines.
- o Createspace paperback cover images must follow the template guidelines. In particular, the bottom-right of the back cover must be reserved for the barcode, which will be added automatically by Createspace. Do not leave a white area for the barcode to go. Fill with your back cover image and allow Createspace to overprint with a barcode.
- o Also, Createspace covers should not have crop marks or any other printer's marks.
- o Avoid cover images with a white background. They often look poor on a thumbnail, retailers will add a border for you anyway, and there are sometimes problems with Createspace printing.
- o Painting a cover image and designing a cover are two separate skills. The importance of typography was always key to a good physical book

cover, but with the significance of thumbnail images, it is even more vital now, possibly more so than the image. Of course, in a great cover, the titling and the picture fit together so well you would not consider them to be anything other than part of the same image. Do bear this in mind as I have seen a number of covers where a great image is ruined by weak typography. When looking for artists, try to find someone who can handle both skills.

MORE ON MARGINS

With regard to page margins, earlier in this book [PAGE LAYOUT p52] I suggested sticking to the Createspace template page setup defaults for novels. For most books, the defaults work well so why change them? For other books the defaults aren't right and so you it will help you to understand a little about margins so you can set them yourself.

Margins aren't difficult to understand, but whenever I just pop into the Createspace site to check the margin guidelines and look for recommendations in the Community forums, I am reminded of how something that is really very simple causes more confusion that it deserves to. So I've written this section to de-mystify.

Let me start by telling you the simplest way to think about margins. Once we've done that, I'll move onto some of the other terms you will hear and why you will hear them. I'm going to assume for now that we're talking here about a standard fiction novel of 200-500 pages that does not use the option to extend the print to the very edge of the page (i.e. is not full bleed).

- Each page has four margins: top and bottom margins are as simple as they sound. You also have an *inner margin* (between the edge of the page that disappears into the binding and the start of the area where text is printed) and an *outer margin* (from the end of the text area to the outer edge of the paper). If you bring up the Page Setup dialog in Word, you will see *inside* margin, not *inner*. Bear with me, we'll come to that. I'm using general terms here rather than Word-specific.

- Notice I said inner and outer margins, and not left and right. Open up a paperback book and you will see a page on the right (a 'facing' page) with the inner margin (disappearing into the binding) on the left side of the page. You will also see a page on the left with its inner margin (disappearing into the binding) on the *right*. Don't worry, there's a diagram coming in a minute...

- If you're wondering about *gutter margins*, don't! Gutter margins don't need to exist as far as you're concerned. In the Microsoft Word Page Setup, set gutter margin to zero. All you need to think about is the *inner margin,*

- You don't see the inside edge of the paper because it's eaten by the binding. And some of the inner part of the page is visible but doesn't lie flat because it is bent sharply into the binding. *The more pages you have, the more of the inner edge of the sheet appears to be consumed by the binding.*

- If you want the text area of the page to look evenly surrounded by margins (which is generally a good idea), then it follows that the inner margin should be larger than the outer margin. That is because you must 'give up' some of the inner portion of the sheet to accommodate the binding.

- And so you need *mirrored margins*. The inner margin needs to be on the left for all facing pages (odd numbered), and on the right for all non-facing pages. Take a look at a physical book and you will see the truth of this.

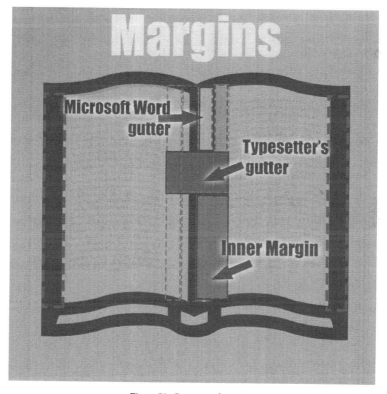

Figure 70: Gutters and margins

Here's a diagram where I've shown some different types of margin.

I said you should concentrate on the *inner margin*. If you're viewing this book in color, that's in the diagram in the light-brown color. In Microsoft Word

PART 7 — ADVANCED TOPICS

terminology, what I've called the inner margin consists of Word's inside margin + Word's gutter margin. In Microsoft Word, gutter margin is an additional margin that runs between the inside margin and the inside edge of the page.

In a bound book, some of the inner margin will appear as a margin, and some will disappear into the binding. In order for the margins in the bound book to *appear* equal either side of the text, the inside margin actually has to be wider than the outside one, as with the diagram.

By adding their gutter margin setting, Microsoft are trying to be helpful. Their idea of the gutter margin is to set aside space on the page to cover the binding so that the remaining inside margin can be set to the same width as the outside margin (to make them balance). Most people I have discussed this don't find this helps them to think about margins, which is why I recommend setting the gutter to zero so you have one fewer setting to fiddle with and think about.

Which leads us finally to what I've called in the diagram *Typesetter's Gutter*. If you hang around the Createspace Community pages (the forums) then you will come across a fair number of regular (and very helpful) contributors who come from the traditional typesetting profession. They will talk about the gutter as begin the inner gap between the text area on *both* pages. This is the traditional meaning of the term 'gutter' in typesetting. I've shaded this in green.

As for Createspace themselves, their guidance seems to use the term *gutter* and *inner margin* interchangeably, even though in their Word templates they set values for both inner and gutter margins.

See, I told you it was overcomplicated!

So, to summarize:

- Always use mirrored margins.

- If your book is a standard novel (in terms of formatting and length) then stick to the Createspace defaults (which I've shown below).

- If you want to set your own margins. Set the gutter margin in Word to zero and just use the inside margin.

- If you read people talking about how they've set margins, be very cautious because people use the terms *inside margin, inner margin* and *gutter margin* to mean different things.

How to choose the inside margin size

Here are the current guidelines from Createspace.

Page Count	Inside Margin	Outside Margins
24 to 150 pages	.375″	at least .25″
151 to 400 pages	.75″	at least .25″
401 to 600 pages	.875″	at least .25″
> 600 pages	1.0″	at least .25″

By 'inside margin' I'm certain Createspace is referring to my definition of inside margin: the blue-shaded area in the diagram above.

If you compare with the default page setup coming out of the Createspace (which is a 0.75″ + .0.13″ = 0.88″ inner margin) then that looks right for a typical novel of around 425 pages. On the other hand, use your common sense in scenarios such as the big jump between 0.375″ and 0.75″ at around 150 pages in this table. A 0.75″ inner margin at 151 pages will look large and won't balance well against a 0.25″ outer margin.

If you are unsure what will look good, it's worth playing around in advance of your publication by trying out a few margin settings (and fonts, font size, and leading/ line height) and printing a test project. You can put a different margin setting in each Word section (the page setup can be set independently for each section. [See the chapter on sections p89].) To see the true effect of margins, though, you will need to change the page count, because large page counts mean more of the page is snaffled by the binding.

CREATESPACE VS. LULU & LSI. WHICH IS BEST?

This is a frequently asked question. That's good because you can google for text such as "createspace or lulu" (keep those quote marks in your Google search) and find a lot of information. One of the first things you'll realize is that there are several other print on demand suppliers too.

You'll notice I haven't provided an answer. Here's why: the print on demand suppliers are in competition with each other. Their services, costs, and formatting and proofing tools change all the time. For example, while I was writing the first edition of this book, Createspace stopped charging for their Pro Plan service. So as you investigate your choice of supplier, consider these points:

- What book format do you want? Lulu currently provides more unusual options, such as spiral-bound.
- Do a cost analysis at latest prices. Createspace tends to be cheaper than Lulu, but Lulu often provides discounts. Think about how you expect to sell your books. Will you sell them yourself by hand, or through an online store? If the latter, then Createspace will often give better margins, but if you are a UK author, you will have to pay 30% tax on your profits unless you register for a US tax number.
- If you read someone online complain about (or praise) the print quality from a particular supplier, look at the date the comment was made, and bear in mind that commenters will often refer to bad experiences they had years ago. In general, I am convinced that the quality of print on demand books has increased significantly over the past decade. The only way to truly compare the print quality of Createspace, Lulu, and the others, is to get your book printed at all of them and compare the results. Even then, the POD suppliers will change printers over time, and the printers will change technology.
- With Createspace, you will automatically get a listing at amazon.com and amazon.co.uk. That automatic listing at amazon.co.uk has only been true since 2012 and the lack of that listing used to be major reason for UK authors to use Lulu. No longer.
- With Lulu (using the free *extendedREACH*) you will get the book on both amazon.com and amazon.co.uk but the process takes longer (several weeks rather than a few days with Createspace). I have heard many people say that Lulu works fine, if you are happy with the wait.

However, a few people do report problems getting their Lulu books listed on amazon at all, or that the book is listed, but with a 2-3 week expected delivery time.

- If you want to publish through both Createspace **and** Lulu, then I'm not aware of any reason to stop you, although you might end up with both a Createspace edition and a (probably more expensive) Lulu edition on amazon.com and possibly elsewhere.

- As a UK author, if you sell books through Createspace, you will be charged 30% witholding tax unless you have registered for a US tax number, something that can take a while, though you can request Createspace to withhold payment of your royalties while you get your tax sorted out. I wrote a blog post explaining how I got my US tax number here https://timctaylor.wordpress.com/2012/05/18/how-uk-authors-can-escape-us-withholding-tax-on-their-royalties./

- Another printer that needs to be mentioned is Lightning Source International (LSI). I know of small publishers who have put their back catalog onto LSI and are pleased with the results. I've not used them myself, but from discussions with publishers who have, costs are higher than with Createspace for small print runs, and stock levels reported through Amazon are sometimes worse than Createspace (e.g. 'book ships in 2-3 weeks') but the quality is slightly higher in terms of paper stock. Also, LSI expect a more direct contact with you and are really set up for small publishers rather than new self-publishers. Australian self-publishers, and those looking to sell to the Australian market, note that LSI now operates out of Melbourne.

ADVANCED COLORSPACES AND DOT GAIN

I'm going to briefly cover some terms you may come across regarding images, though they apply to more than just images: dot gain and colorspaces. For our purposes, the terms apply to the way in which the PDF files for your book's interior and its cover tell the printing machine that makes your book how to handle color and how to handle grayscales and black. This applies to text but most importantly to images.

Also, way back toward the start of this part of the book on images, I mentioned that in traditional publishing, photographs would be bound separately on glossy paper stock. I deliberately skipped over the reason why until now.

For 99% of the readers of this book, there is no need to understand the concepts I describe in this section. But since the first edition of this book has sold several thousand copies, that 1% means I have readers who could benefit from this new chapter. For the other 99%, if you read on you might gain a basic understanding of a few concepts that give a deeper understanding of printing, but if you have a copy of Adobe Acrobat or running Mac OS, you should resist the urge to fiddle with the default settings in your PDF. With Createspace, the guide is always that if your printed proof copy looks good, leave your book alone, and if it doesn't, try asking around on Createspace Community forums, ring Createspace support, and produce private printings to try out various approaches.

Many of the tools for manipulating color spaces are only available outside of Microsoft Word. Images can be manipulated in Gimp or Adobe Photoshop before inserting into Word. PDF ink and color profile settings may be available in your PDF printer driver (certainly the case with Macs) or PDF exporter, and certainly in Adobe Acrobat Pro.

First of all, I'll describe the concepts. Then I'll move on to problems and possible solutions.

Cast your mind to Coca Cola. I'm sure you know the logo: white text on a red background. That's a very specific red. If you see the logo on a website, or on a can, on the label of a plastic bottle, a mirror, a coffee mug, on a corporate letterhead, on your TV screen or in a glossy color book about classic logo design, or in the black-and-white paperback edition of the same book, the red should look exactly the same in all cases (except the paperback, of course).

Many different printing techniques will be used to achieve the same red color on all those backdrops. The computer display, tablet, and TV images will be different again, because the display technology to mix colored lights to fire into your eye is fundamentally different from the printing technologies that mix dyes and pigments to absorb colors out of ambient white light (which is why your computer monitor is often a poor guide to how images will appear in your paperback book).

The way in which that color is encoded (for example in a jpg image file or text in a PDF document) is called a COLOR SPACE.

Mixing colored lights is called an *additive* process. You start off with black (i.e. your monitor/ TV/ tablet/ smartphone before it is switched on) and then each pixel on your display is either left blank or has a combination of red, green and blue light mixed together. This is called the RGB color model. There are actually several different schemes for RGB color, but the most common by far is called sRGB. In terms of your PDF that Createspace uses, this is called the sRGB COLORSPACE.

Mixing colored inks is a *subtractive* process. You start off with white (or near white) paper and white-ish ambient light and mix colored inks that have the effect of taking colors out of the white light. For example, mixing cyan and magenta inks makes blue. What happens here is that you see blue wavelengths of light because the inks absorb all the other wavelengths (they have been subtracted from the white light hitting the page).

Just as each pixel in an SRGB colorspace image is described as an amount of red, green, and blue, each pixel in a colorspace used for mixing colored inks is described in terms of how much of each ink to use for that pixel. The most common way to do this is with the CMYK color model. If you have an inkjet printer, that's what it will use. The C, Y, and M stand for cyan, yellow and magenta, and the K is for black (because black ink is cheaper and in some situations gives better printing results than mixing C Y and M to achieve black).

You will see me move between the terms COLOR MODEL and COLOR SPACE. A color space is a specific implementation of a color model. You may come across COLOR PROFILE too, which essentially means the same as color space.

If you use Adobe products you may come across yet another term WORKING SPACE. I've never been entirely clear on that term but I think the idea comes from Adobe Photoshop and reflects the idea of an input color space (for example for your camera) a working space which is the color model currently used by your image while it is being edited, and then an output color space which is mindful of how it will be printed or displayed.

If this seems like a lot of detail, that's because it is. And I haven't even finished with color spaces as there's still more to come later. One of the things I'm doing here is arming you with basic concepts so that if you need to talk with people in the Createspace community, you at least have a grasp of the basics. Once you have the concepts you will find there is a lot more information available online that you now know the terms to Google for and the basic concepts to understand what you find.

Another term you may come across is SPOT COLOR. This means ink that is pre-mixed to a specific color rather than mixed on the fly from a combination of cyan, magenta and yellow (and sometimes orange and green too). For example, I worked for a corporation called ICI and remember when our team received a severe telling off for the way we had produced an in-house office newsletter. Our crime was that we had used the wrong blue in the corporate logo. If the blue was not specifically Pantone 294, then we must not use the ICI logo at all! Pantone is another colorspace, by the way, and I have no doubt that ICI corporate printing used Pantone 294 as a spot color, just as Coca Cola will use a red spot color for theirs. The most likely reason you might be interested in spot color with Createspace is whether in some case you might want to adjust the PDF to use black spot color rather than achieving black by mixing cyan, magenta, yellow and black (mixing all the inks is called 'rich black'), or by doing the reverse.

Adjusting spot colors and rich blacks is only possible with PDF editing facilities, such as Adobe Acrobat Pro, and is the kind of voodoo that is best avoided except as a last resort. And it is voodoo because Createspace will not tell us the printing process that they use. All the same, I have fixed problems with overly gray text by swapping rich blacks for solid black spot color.

Grayscale colorspaces and Dot Gain

We've talked so far about color. Most of you will have a black and white book interior. What appears as gray shades and colors in your Word manuscript will appear to come out as shades of gray in the book. In fact, that is an illusion as your book will only be printed in black ink. If an image appears to be in shades of gray, look very closely, and you will see the 'gray ink' is actually made up of little black dots. Bigger dots closer together make for a darker shade of gray.

If all is working well, the dots are very small and you will need to peer very closely to see them.

The term DOT GAIN refers to the way in which ink seeps into the page. With what appears to be gray actually consisting of little black dots, the paper used to print on makes a big difference. With the kind of normal paper stock used for pages of a mass market novel, for example, the ink of the black dots seeps into the surrounding area. This increase in size of the dots is the dot gain.

For black and white printing, the most common grayscale profiles (color space) are based on this idea of dot gain. For example, a common profile is 'dot gain 20%'. This is an attempt to compensate for the seepage. The default dot gain is usually 20%. You will also see grayscale profiles called 'gray gamma'. These are for display screens, not printing.

I mentioned elsewhere in the book that traditionally printed books with photographs will often use separate glossy paper for the photographs. This is because the dot gain will be less on the glossier paper (less seep) and also to some degree because the images will look sharper on white paper. With Createspace you don't get that option. To freely mix text and graphics and photos is liberating, but starts from a position of not having the option to use the highest quality photo paper. I have to say, though, that in my experience you can produce high quality grayscale images using standard Createspace paper. Yes, the might look a little sharper if each image is manipulated beforehand according to its need by an expert (for example, by reducing the tonal range) but for most types of book, your readers will not notice the difference. The quality feel of paper stock used in the cover and interior is likely to make more difference to the reader than the nuances of whether to convert images to 8-bit monochrome or DeviceGray colorspace.

What should I do with my color sRGB images for my black and white paperback?

The short answer is leave them alone.

For images inside your book, most people will have jpg or png format images in sRGB colorspace. Below is what a typical jpg file will look like if you right-click | properties from Windows File Explorer.

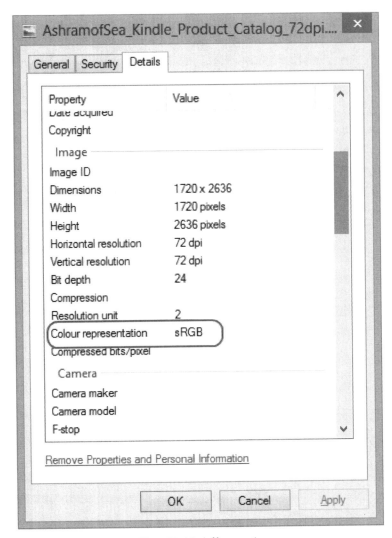

Figure 71: A jpg's file properties

If you start with color sRGB images and want to produce a black and white book interior with Createspace, the simplest solution is for you to leave them alone. Createspace will adjust them for you according to their needs. The same is true for your color cover or if you produce a color paperback interior.

Other printers may insist that all images for color printing should be in CMYK and that sRGB images have no place in printing, but this is not the case with Createspace.

There are other ways to manipulate colorspaces and to manipulate images and these will produce slightly different results. However, they are not necessarily *better* results, and for most authors, the simplicity of inserting sRGB images and letting Createspace tweak the knobs and dials of the technical printing process is worth more than the marginal improvements in image quality that might be achieved through other means, but that your readers probably would never notice in any case.

If image quality is absolutely essential to your book then I suggest:

1. Hand your images over to a professional typesetter to manipulate and to create the PDF for you.
2. Expect to have several rounds of proofs and alterations.
3. Consider using a printer other than Createspace who will give you the option of using higher quality paper stock.

Which PDF settings should I use?

That's difficult to answer because it depends on what tools are available to you to generate your PDF, but I can give some rules of thumb.

Createspace PDF Settings: The Basic Rules

Set a high quality print mode (such as the Adobe PDF Maker option for 'High Quality Print'). We're looking for something that does NOT downsize your image resolution.

If you have sRGB color images in your Word document, leave them alone. Do not convert to CMYK.

Avoid PDF/X options unless no other high quality print options are available or you need PDF/X to address other problems

---

That may seem surprising given that PDF/X is billed as a digital printing standard. That's what it is, but it's not Createspace's standard and might lead to unnecessary color space conversion problems (some PDF/X standards insist on converting to CMYK and that's a job better left to Createspace).

Here's why.

I mentioned color models a little earlier. CMYK is a very important color model for printing, but a generic CMYK color space is a theoretical device-independent profile, not one that is actually used by real printing presses, which will use a

DEVICE DEPENDENT COLOR SPACE. Common CMYK device dependent color spaces are 'US Web Coated (SWOP) v2' and 'HP 5000 Semi Matte Exp05'. These are available as software files with extension ".icc". You can download many of them from Adobe.com

The problem comes when your images are converted from one color space to another. Some color spaces can represent more colors than others (they are said to have a wider GAMUT). If your image is converted from a wider color gamut to a narrower one, you may lose color information and that may lead to the wrong colors appearing in the book. The more color space conversions that take place as you move from the original image to the final print process, the more problems you are likely to experience.

What you don't want is to do is transform your native sRGB images into a generic CMYK before uploading to Createspace, only for Createspace to then transform your image again to the device dependent CMYK color space profile that they use with their printing press.

A better default approach is to leave your sRGB images alone. When you create your PDF file, the images will automatically be tagged as being in the sRGB color space. Createspace at their end will know how to convert that to the colorspace used by their printing press. Createspace won't tell you what that colorspace is, so leave that to them.

Incidentally, if you get some printing done by your local printer, and they say they need CMYK, ask what ICC color profile they require. If they're any good, they will give you the .icc file if you don't already have it so they can match your requirements exactly.

So that's the generic answer. That's what I would do in your shoes because I would try simple first and then start fiddling if that didn't work out to my satisfaction.

Cover artwork and CMYK

Some cover artists will deliver cover artwork in a CMYK colorspace. That will produce good results with your paperback cover but is not a mandatory requirement. Some other printers do require images to be provided in CMYK. This is very common for promotional material and adverts in printed magazines.

What you must never do (and I speak from experience here #cringe#) is take a CMYK image and convert it to sRGB. The colors will look wrong. Usually the artist will work in an RGB colorspace until the final production of the file so if you might need an sRGB version, ask your artist for one as well as CMYK.

Why would you need an sRGB image too? Only high-specification graphics packages allow you to edit CMYK images. Adobe Photoshop Elements and GIMP are two popular packages that do not let you work with CMYK images. If you have an online presence as an author you will probably find plenty of occasions where you want to make minor adjustments to your cover artwork for adverts, posters, bookmarks, banners and so on. If your image is CMYK then you can't do this yourself without an expensive graphics package such as Adobe Photoshop.

Problems and solutions

Up to this point I've introduced a large number of concepts and told you essentially not to fiddle with them.

But what if your proof copy does not look good? What if you see banding or ugly great white polka dots in the text of your title page?

If you're running Word under Windows and you don't have a PDF editing tool of the caliber of Adobe Acrobat Pro then you only have the chance to edit your images; if your text doesn't look right then you need to contact a professional typesetter. If you're printing a black and white interior, try (after backing up the originals) converting your sRGB color image to 8-bit monochrome in a graphics package and then re-inserting into Word.

If you have Adobe Acrobat Pro, try Print Production | Preflight Digital Printing and Online Publishing | Digital Printing (B/W) [ensure you use 'analyze and fix'].

Alternatively try changing colorspace options directly. The screenshot below is from Adobe Acrobat Pro's 'Convert Colors' tool under 'Print Production'.

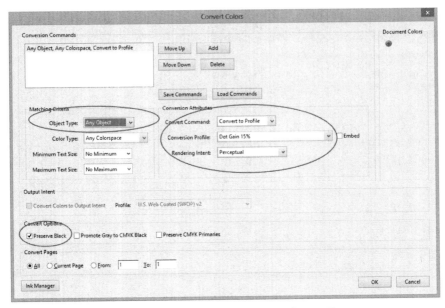

Figure 72: Converting Colors in Adobe Acrobat Pro XI

BEYOND MICROSOFT WORD — IS IT WORTH PAYING FOR ANYTHING ELSE?

There are several expensive software products that can enhance the quality of your paperback by doing things Word cannot. For most people the benefits are marginal and there are better ways to achieve the same ends.

I started this book with a proposition: that you can produce a great paperback with Createspace using nothing more than Microsoft Word. I stand by that.

However, Word has its limitations, and if you are using Word 2007 or earlier then these limitations could be serious if your book needs high quality images. For most people, though, the benefits of extending Word's capabilities by buying other software is minimal. Even if you feel these minimal benefits are worthwhile, unless you are setting up your own publishing or book design business, you would save money and get better results by paying someone else to finish off your manuscript rather than buy software and learn to use it yourself.

In this section, I will go through some of the most common add-on products to Word, and then run through some of Word's limitations.

A note about Adobe products

Since the first edition of this book, Adobe has moved firmly in the direction of software as a service with *Creative Cloud*. I own Adobe software that I've bought as a disk or downloaded, installed on my computer and I can use for the rest of my life (or until it gets too obsolete and I want to upgrade). The current set of products (the CS6 range) are the last versions that Adobe will release in this traditional way. In future the only way to buy new versions of Adobe software is to rent the right to use the software through Creative Cloud. There are winners and losers in this. If you were considering purchasing Adobe software, you might be a winner or loser, but either way you can't ignore this change from Adobe.

Adobe Acrobat Standard/ Pro

You've almost certainly used Adobe Acrobat Reader, it's the free software you use to view PDF files. Adobe has two products that are not free and can be used to build, edit and inspect PDFs. Since PDFs are what ultimately gets sent to the printing press, they are of great interest to us.

For our purposes, Adobe Acrobat Standard embeds itself inside Microsoft Word, and lets you build PDFs using Adobe's PDF-building software. Of course, Word 2007 and later already allows you to build PDFs and Macs since 2007 have this built into OS X, so there has to be something better about Adobe-built PDFs than Microsoft- or Apple-built PDFs to make Acrobat worth buying. In a few cases there are. Before we move on to examine them, a word of warning about versions. You need to be running a version of Adobe Acrobat that matches your version of Word. If you're running Word 2007 or 2008, then you need Adobe Acrobat X or XI. If you're running Word 2013, then Adobe Acrobat X is no use to you, you must be running Adobe Acrobat XI. In other words, if you intend to keep Adobe Acrobat as part of your software setup, then every time you upgrade to a new version of Microsoft Word, expect to also upgrade to a new version of Adobe Acrobat. If you are considering a new purchase, Adobe's Creative Cloud has free upgrades built in to the subscription.

Here are some reasons to buy Adobe Acrobat Standard

There is no limitation to the resolution of images (which is also true of some other third-party PDF tools). If the only image in your book is an author photo in your bio at the end, then this is no big deal. If you're writing a full-color cookbook or illustrated children's story, then this could be the game changer.

The PDF is built by Adobe, not Microsoft or Apple, or any other third party. PDFs are not all created equally. This is not to say that other PDFs are no good, nor that Adobe Acrobat is free from bugs.

It's like this. There used to be a saying in the computer industry: *No one was ever fired for buying IBM*. I build book PDFs for a living. No one is ever going to fire me for building them with Adobe.

Here are some reasons to buy Adobe Acrobat Professional rather than Standard

It lets you produce PDFs to the PDFX/1a standard required by Lightning Source and some other printers. Mac users can print to this standard anyway, as part of Apple's operating system. However, if you are a Windows user, then up to and including Windows 8 running Word 2013, the only way to produce PDFX/1a that I am aware of is through Adobe Acrobat Pro. I've looked at various third-party PDF software and can't see any that claim PDFx/1a capability.

It lets you see inside the PDF, edit it, change it, and run 'preflight checks' including one supplied by Createspace. Now for most people most of the time, there is no need to do this unless there is a problem with your PDF. If there is a problem with your PDF then you're probably better off paying someone to fix it for you rather than buy software to fiddle with settings you don't understand. PDF problems are rare but I've seen text that comes out gray, even though the font is set to black in Microsoft Word. I've seen images that look fine in Word gain white polka dots in the PDF. These sorts of problems aren't easy to fix because they require knowledge of some concepts new to Word users, and there's something of the 'dark arts' about this because we don't know what printing settings Createspace uses and they refuse to tell us (with good reason, to be fair).

PDF Editing in Word for Windows 2013

When I first heard of new facilities to edit PDFs in Word 2013, I thought it might be a game changer, something that meant there was no longer a need to buy Adobe Acrobat for editing. I was disappointed. To some degree you can extract a Word document out of a PDF, a facility that Adobe Acrobat already provides. It's ugly but possibly better than printing the PDF and scanning it in through OCR.

More importantly, I was hoping that Microsoft's attention on PDFs would mean that finally you could create PDFs that don't automatically reduce the resolution of all images. Unfortunately there is no change from Word 2010. Microsoft's PDF export reduces image resolution to 199dpi. There's no way around this.

Working around the faults in Adobe Acrobat

For we Microsoft Word users, the best way to make PDFs is from the button Adobe embeds inside the Word Ribbon. Unfortunately it doesn't always work. Certainly I've produced faulty PDFs through Adobe Acrobat Pro X and XI. Luckily, there is a workaround. If you get a faulty PDF (usually manifesting itself as tiny fonts at 1pt or smaller, text inside margins, or faint ghosting around images) then instead of making the PDF from the 'Create PDF' button Adobe embeds in the Ribbon, instead print from Word using the PDF printer driver that Adobe creates.

Paying someone to run Adobe Acrobat for you

If you're like me, you would like to do all of the work yourself. It's more satisfying. But if your Word document is fine, but you are being let down by Word's PDF export tool consider asking author communities for a recommendation for a reliable book formatter and ask the formatter whether they can simply use their Adobe Acrobat to build your PDF from the Word document you supply. They should offer a deep discount on their normal fee as they aren't actually going to do any layout work.

Adobe InDesign

Summary: Adobe InDesign is a great tool for adding the final steps of showroom polish to your book layout. However, seen in a cold, commercial light, most authors would be better spending their time and money elsewhere.

Adobe InDesign is the leading product for typesetters in the major publishing houses. There are rival products too, but if you take a selection of printed books off your bookshelf, I would guess that more of them have been produced using Adobe InDesign than anything else.

The workflow for using InDesign would be to write your book in Microsoft Word as normal, and then import the Word file into InDesign for the final layout. InDesign is not a word processor; you don't write there, although minor corrections to the text are possible if, for example, you have a spelling mistake.

So what can InDesign do for you?

- Better hyphenation and HORIZONTAL JUSTIFICATION.
- TRUE SMALLCAPS rather than faux smallcaps.
- Export an EBOOK EDITION (semi) automatically

HORIZONTAL JUSTIFICATION involves shuffling the words around inside a text box until the right hand side of the last character of the last word on a wrapped line butts up against the right edge of the text box. If that's confusing, go back to the image on [p113] to remind yourself. Or... if you're reading the paperback version of this book, just look at the current page as an example of justification.

Sometimes the words don't fit as neatly as you would like. This is especially true of lines with lengthy words and of narrow columns (such as newspapers). Go take some novels off your bookshelf. You will see that most of the ones from traditional publishing houses will have a few lines where the last word on a line is split across two lines, being joined by a hyphen.

With good hyphenation, you won't normally notice the words are being broken. With bad hyphenation, you will throw the book to the ground and jump up and down on the poor thing. The key to good hyphenation is to have a good *hyphenation dictionary* — a set of rules for where you can break specific words across lines. Adobe InDesign has a good hyphenation dictionary. I'm not so sure about Word's, though.

Is hyphenation worth doing? I've tested this and some other layout design choices out on some unsuspecting volunteers who weren't told in advance what they were looking for. The results were that with a novel of a roughly standard layout, normal people don't notice the difference between well-hyphenated justified layout and un-hyphenated justified layout. It might be that good hyphenation makes the lines on the page just that little bit easier to read, but not at a level readers would be conscious of.

Put it another way, with hyphenation you run the risk of making your book look terrible if you get it wrong, but if you get it right, the prize is... *very few people will notice anyway!*

Did you?

I'm typing these words into a Microsoft Word 2013 .docx file which has not been set to use hyphenation, except for the section you are currently reading. I have hyphenated this section using Word's automatic hyphenation (which is under the Page Layout section of the Ribbon). I've left the rest of the book unhyphenated. Could you tell?

You were more likely to notice if you are reading an eBook edition of this book. The text of the eBook editions was copied from Word into Notepad++, a code editor; from there I coded the book using html and css. Guess what? All those hyphens that Word put in to produce neat justification come through to Notepad++ as hyphens and will come through all the way to the eBook version readers see on their Kindles, Nooks, iPads or whatever. But when Word added the hyphen, it knew exactly where the line wrapped. In an eBook I cannot possibly know where your lines will wrap. Almost certainly not in the same place as the paperback. And that means the hyphens will look truly awful and very noticeable.

I've deliberately made my eBook look bad so you don't do the same. When I weigh up the pros and cons I struggle to see the justification (sorry) of hyphenation when you risk disaster for such tenuous benefits.

Normal people don't notice hyphenation in standard books. That's what I wrote a little earlier and I'd better finish by defining *normal* and *standard*.

By 'normal people' I mean those people who might buy your book and also the people most likely to review it. If your paperback has the wrong font, a confused front matter, insufficient leading, or an indentation for the first line of each chapter, then a significant number of reviewers will spot this and mark you down for poor formatting. But very few reviewers will notice your lack of hyphenation, or your use of faux small caps, for that matter.

Professional typographers *will* notice. But the only reason why *you* will notice professional typographers is because you will find them blogging about book layouts (often to sell you their services) or hanging around places such as the Createspace Community forums. So listen to their advice (which is often sound on many topics and generously offered) but remember two points when you read what typographers have to say online:

- Unless you are writing a book about typography, they will be an infinitesimally small portion of the target market for your books.
- Most of them have worked with tools such as Adobe InDesign and Adobe Acrobat Pro for many years. Many of them are dismissive of using Microsoft Word to do anything other than basic wordprocessing and are ignorant of what Word can and cannot do.

As for 'standard book', I'm thinking of novels and most poetry and non-fiction. The place where you are most likely to benefit from hyphenation and the layout controls of InDesign is where you have multi-column page layouts or floated images with narrow columns of text running beside the images.

We discussed true smallcaps earlier (see page [220]) and that Word uses faux small caps (unless you pick them one-by-one from INSERT | SYMBOL).

InDesign can use proper small cap glyphs. Is this a reason to buy InDesign (or, indeed, Microsoft Publisher)?

That's a subjective question. I would say no. The purpose of small caps is to make text look distinctive so that it stands out, ideally in an elegant way, and also in a way that looks good when combined in the same paragraph as body text. I've deliberately demonstrated this in my use of small caps in this section.

I introduced this section by stating there were several things InDesign can do for you, and I put the key words in small caps: HORIZONTAL JUSTIFICATION, TRUE SMALL CAPS and EBOOKS. Rather than use each of these four features as sub-sub-headings, I have put each key word in small caps (and bold) where it appears in the narrative. This is a reference work, which means people will scan looking for a specific fragment of text in a way they wouldn't with a novel. This small cap technique makes it easy to scan for and find the text you want.

Of course, I could have presented those features as lower level headings, but this can break up the text into stuttering bullet points, and once you have more than two levels of heading lower that chapter headings, then it can be very easy to lose track of what level you are at.

The important thing here is that I feel the small caps in this section aren't there to look pretty, they are performing a useful function *even though they are faux small caps*. Yes, all the small caps in this book are faux small caps. If you're reading the paperback version, the font is Palatino Linotype, a font supplied by Windows 8 and available to me typing these words in Word 2013. I think the faux small caps still perform their task perfectly well.

This book explains how to layout the interior of a paperback, but most self-publishing authors looking to sell their books will sell more copies in EBOOK EDITIONS. While you can upload Word documents directly to some retailer and aggregator sites, such as Amazon KDP and Smashwords, many features of eBooks are not available or are likely to go wrong through that route, such as floating text around images.

InDesign allows export to the ePUB eBook format. Amazon also provides a beta version of a plug-in for InDesign that allows export to the Kindle format. This Amazon plug-in broke in 2012 when Amazon updated their Kindle reader firmware. Even Amazon's own documentation for their InDesign plug in became barely readable. The Kindle plug-in may be working by the time you read this, but those problems with the plug-in mean that I would hesitate to ever use it myself.

There are plenty of online guides about how to produce ePUB books from InDesign. It's tricky and there are easier and I think better ways to produce eBooks, but it can be done.

I'm not saying you shouldn't use Adobe InDesign as part of your eBook building. What I'm saying is that you should not buy InDesign with the expectation that because you are buying an expensive product it will au-tomagically produce good quality eBooks and protect you from the need to understand how to code eBooks. As I write these words in summer 2013, the eBooks produced today by major publishing houses are mostly of acceptable quality. Until recently, though, most of the worst formatted eBooks I bought came from major publishers, and I believe the biggest cause is that layout teams were running Adobe InDesign and thought that if they built their eBook editions from InDesign then that was all they needed to do. Wrong!

IN CONCLUSION, I've spent several pages explaining about InDesign. I've done that in part because this book is about advising you to lay out interiors for paperbacks you publish at Createspace. InDesign can do things with interior layout that Microsoft Word cannot. I assert and continue to assert that you can produce great looking books without needing InDesign, so I have had to justify myself here.

The other reason I've dwelt on InDesign is because the part of me that likes to make things *wants* it. I've trialed InDesign, played with it, considered adding it to my book production workflow on numerous occasions. Every time, though, my commercial side kicks in and asks whether InDesign will help me to earn money to feed my family. The answer is 'no'. Here's why...

Adobe InDesign can add finishing touches of quality to your interior layout that are beyond Microsoft Word's capabilities. You would need to make a considerable investment of time and money to learn how to use InDesign effectively. Unfortunately, all this investment is unlikely to lead to a single additional book sale.

Adobe Photoshop

Adobe Photoshop is an image editing, painting, photo-compositing application. I've used Photoshop CS6 in producing this book, but I've used free equivalents Paint.net and Gimp more. If you're wanting to produce high quality images for a front cover or designing your brand logo, then Photoshop does have many advantages over Gimp and Paint.net, but you will need to put in a lot of work to learn how to perform even simple tasks.

For me, the key reason to move to Photoshop CS6 was because I needed to edit files in CMYK colorspace. You are unlikely to need that. If your need for images is to tidy up an old photo for your biography page, or to shrink some cover images for a 'other books by...' page, then a free tool such as Paint.net is all you need.

CutePDF Writer

The basic version, that works as a simple PDF printer driver, is free. Like many other cheap PDF printer drivers, it doesn't actually create the PDF file itself, but is more of a wrapper for the freeware Postscript to PDF tools such as Ghostscript. There are Pro versions that let you do more but nothing necessary for printing to Createspace.

doPDF

A PDF printer driver. Does the basic tasks well, including setting image dpi up to 1200dpi and flexible page sizes. Is free, but more facilities in a paid version (such as setting hyperlinks in your PDF file; all things that are useful in an office environment, but not useful for our use with Createspace).

Nitro Pro

A PDF tool that compares itself to Adobe Acrobat Pro for less than half the price tag ($120 last I looked). Does a lot more than simply create PDF files.

NovaPDF

Another PDF driver I've seen and heard recommended. Currently costs $40-$50 depending on which version you buy. You can download a free trial version.

Scrivener

Like yWriter5, Scrivener is a tool for assembling a book. Microsoft Word has outlining, which can help, but Word is really set up to be one big file for everything. Scrivener and yWriter5 divide your book up into scenes, characters, and locations and gives you more options for organizing and thinking about your work that Word can offer. I've not used Scrivener in anger, but plenty of people have, so look around online for writers giving their experiences and their tips. The product costs $40 last time I looked, and is available in Windows and MacOS editions.

I've taken Scrivener files from clients in order for me to build eBooks, so I've had to look into how Scrivener works and I'm impressed! The manual is up to date, professional, and informative, and the software is improving all the time.

Although my connection with Scrivener has been to build eBooks from Scrivener files, you can create PDFs through Scrivener, as well as eBooks in ePUB and Kindle format. People have said good things about the Scrivener-generated eBooks and the eBook code looks fairly clean to me. The reason I get called in is where authors have complex or special requirements that defeat even the best eBook auto-generators.

yWriter5

Like Scrivener, yWriter5 is designed for you to assemble novels through scenes, locations, items, notes and characters, rather than lumping everything into one large Word document. It is only available for Windows and is free (though please donate if you use it). I have used yWriter5 (and yWriter4) to write novels and think it's excellent. However, with all the investment and good reviews I hear about Scrivener, I would consider the other product the next time I write a series of novels.

TEXT BOXES AND WORDART

Microsoft Word is a wordprocessor and not a tool for laying out full-bleed, color graphics for corporate brochures, lavishly illustrated cookbooks or an illustrated children's encyclopedia. Yet Word does have the ability to create graphical images on the page and arrange text around them. In fact, it sometimes sits uncomfortably in the Microsoft Office product lineup on the Windows platform by stealing the thunder of Microsoft Publisher, which is the product Microsoft would prefer you buy to produce your corporate brochures etc.

I'm going to show you some of what Word is capable of in a moment, but let's set expectations first:

- Although its layout capabilities are good, Word is never going to be as good at producing artwork as, say, Adobe Photoshop.
- The artwork you create in Word can look superb, but check as soon as you can how it will look in PDF format. In the translation to PDF, sometimes smooth edges can become jagged and other strange effects can occur.
- Even where Word has the capability, it doesn't mean that you personally have the skills to translate that into a great graphical layout. If you hire someone else to do the graphical layout, they will not only bring the tools but also the experience and flair for creating great designs that pop out of the page.

Okay, now we've got that out of the way, I'm going to show you an example of what Word can do using SHAPES, TEXT BOXES and WORDART. I've put together a menu for a zombie fast food outlet. It's not great artwork, and I gave myself a time limit of 45 minutes, but it serves as an example to talk about.

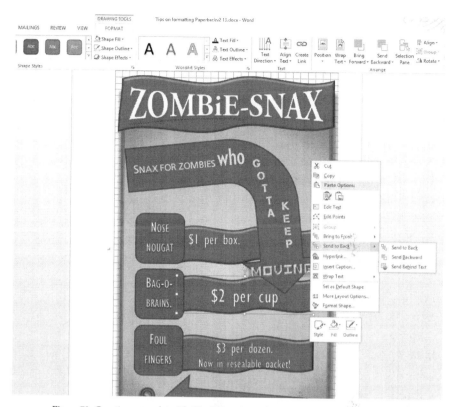

Figure 73: Creating artwork inside Word 2013. Note the DRAWING TOOLS Ribbon menu.

If I were doing this for real, I would add in some images, and I'd use Adobe Photoshop to wrap the text along the arrow that curves downward. But for this exercise I didn't want to use any tool other than Microsoft Word. I'm using Word 2013 here. The drawing tools haven't changed essentially since Word 2007, though with each new version of Word, they get incremental improvements.

First off, some concepts.

PRESETS are a concept Microsoft introduced to its drawing tools in Word 2007, and they are a lifesaver. If you play around with text effects, shape fill, shape styles etc, you will see a lot of settings you can set yourself such as transparency, blur, angle, distance. You will also see preset buttons because Microsoft has selected some great looks for you. Play around and see what you like. I rarely use anything other than presets except to select color and gradients.

The arrows, boxes and ribbons on my zombie poster are SHAPES. TEXT BOXES are a simple kind of shape too. All of them have the concept of FILLS, which simply means what colors in the background of the shape. You can have nothing at all (as with most of my text boxes in the example), or a solid color, a GRADIENT between two or more colors, or a pattern. In the example I've gone for solid color except for the background rectangle that fills the page. For this I used a gradient fill and designed my own gradient of putrid orange, purple and nicotine-stained paper, as befits a zombie fast(-ish) food company.

Figure 74: Advanced shape editing

If you drill down through the menus, you will see that most elements, even text and box outlines, can take GRADIENTS rather than solid colors. Gradients are simply blends of more than one color. Defining your own gradient is something that Microsoft has enhanced with each version, and by Word 2013 it's pretty much on a par with Adobe Photoshop. With the background to the zombie menu (which is a text box), I selected TEXT FILL and edited the gradient by clicking several times on the GRADIENT STOPS bar. Usually you want a subtle blend between closely related colors, but here I added a red and purple stop. This tells Word to blend the colors between each neighboring stop on the gradient stops bar. By the way, if you're reading this in black and white, you can see key images from the book in color at my website: www.timctaylor.com

Shapes and text boxes have OUTLINES, which means the border around the outside of the shape. Most other software calls these strokes. You have control over color, pattern, and transparency, and can set the shape to NO FILL, which is what I did here with many of the text boxes.

All the shapes can be ROTATED. Click on the shape to select it and then to rotate, drag the rotating arrow icon (Word 2013) or green circle (Word 2007/10).

Back to my example — the text for the curving arrow at the top and the left-pointing arrow at the bottom was placed using multiple text boxes. Each text box was set to no outline and no fill, so all we see is the text.

The ear is a symbol from the Webdings font. I created a text box, selected Insert Symbol, and hunted through Webdings until I found something to insert.

The left-pointing arrow is from INSERT SHAPES, which you find to the left of the DRAWING TOOLS Ribbon menu. Microsoft only provides a right-pointing arrow, so I selected the arrow shape and clicked on the rotation arrow above the selection to rotate until it pointed left. Unfortunately this made the text appear upside down. So I deleted the text and reapplied it with a new text box set to no fill and no outline.

Finally, the ordering of elements in the text boxes and shapes can be vital. In our zombie example, the ZOMBIE-SNAX banner at the top must sit on top of the background rectangle and not underneath. Word uses a concept of stacking its displayed objects. It's like having a stack of cut out card shapes arranged on top of each other on a table with you looking down from above. You see the shapes at the top and they obscure objects underneath. Common sense, really. To set the order of an object in the stack, you right click and SEND BACKWARD/ FORWARD. (I'm doing that in the screenshot you've just seen).

While fun to play with, most of these techniques aren't relevant to your average fiction book. But it's worth exploring what can be done as on occasion it can be useful. For example I used Word's built-in drawing tools (actually a 'SmartArt' shape) to create a timeline for a science fiction collection of short stories set in the same universe.

THE SKYFIRE CHRONICLES

Timeline of events and stories

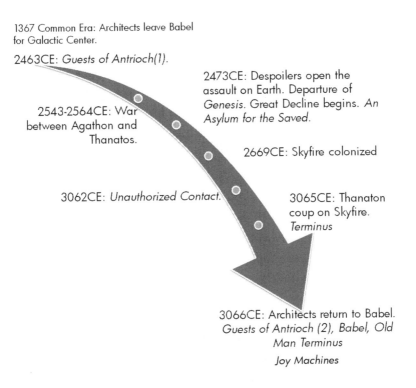

1367 Common Era: Architects leave Babel for Galactic Center.

2463CE: *Guests of Antrioch(1)*.

2473CE: Despoilers open the assault on Earth. Departure of *Genesis*. Great Decline begins. *An Asylum for the Saved*.

2543-2564CE: *War between Agathon and Thanatos*.

2669CE: Skyfire colonized

3062CE: *Unauthorized Contact*.

3065CE: Thanaton coup on Skyfire. *Terminus*

3066CE: Architects return to Babel. *Guests of Antrioch (2), Babel, Old Man Terminus*

Joy Machines

Figure 75: Actual example of Word art

Wordart & Text Effects

WORDART changed with Word 2007 to become more professional looking and bound to all the other forms of font styling (such as italics and underlines) rather than a separate entity as it was with Word 2003. In fact, in Word 2010/2013 you can access Wordart styles directly from the Font menu area of the Ribbon (see image on next page) and the TEXT EFFECTS... button at the bottom of the Font dialog (see image to the right). Microsoft are a little confused because sometimes they use the term Wordart and sometimes they refer to Text Effects, but they mean the same thing: the shadows, glows, outlining, beveling and reflections that

Figure 77: Text effects (direct formatting)

can really lift out text to make it special in text boxes and the like.

Text effects can also look good with titles. I added a shadow text effect to the subtitle for this section. You can get problems with shadows, though, when the canvas for the shadow extends much wider than you think, and crosses into the wrong side of the margin. Interior Reviewer can complain.

If you want to define text effects as part of a style, you can't do it using the Font dialog, you have to pick Text Effects from the Format button at the bottom of the Modify Styles dialog (see screenshot to the left).

Text effects can be powerful, but are best left off body text.

Figure 76: Text effects (styles)

If you're reading this section in an eBook edition you may be seeing shadows and other text effects. If so, they are nothing to do with Microsoft Word, eBook text styles are achieved through something called CSS styling.

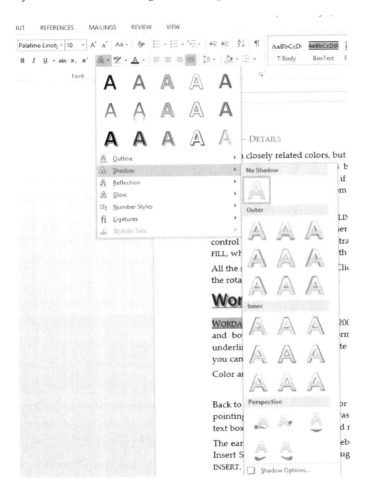

Figure 78: Text Effects directly from the Ribbon in Word 2013. Note the access to OpenType font features, such as Number Styles and Ligatures under the text effects. See the topic on OpenType.

WHERE TO FIND FURTHER INFORMATION

There is a wealth of material on the internet to help you with formatting, self-publishing and writing in general. Unfortunately some of it is misguided and some is out of date. So try to get multiple opinions on a topic, and check the date of the post. Here are some sites to get you started.

The website for this book

I have a page on my website dedicated to this book, where I will post updates and additional guidance. Feel free to leave a comment to ask a question, or just to say, 'hi'. There's a button at the top-right of my website for you to subscribe to my blog. This means you will get an email whenever I post a new topic, to save you having to visit to find whether I've posted an update. Most blogs have something similar, so a good idea is to pick a few publishing and writing blogs you like and subscribe to them.

http://timctaylor.wordpress.com/format-your-book-for-createspace/

Createspace and Lulu community support

Both sites have forums where you can post and answer questions. This is extremely valuable as the question you want to ask has probably been asked before.

Createspace: https://www.createspace.com/en/community/index.jspa

Lulu: http://connect.lulu.com/t5/Lulu-Connect-Self-publishing-and/ct-p/en_US

Book design & Typography Sites

I recommend TheBookDesigner.com where Joel Friedlander shares a lot that is worth paying attention to on all aspects of print and eBook self-publishing, with a particular passion for typography. Joel is good at sharing links to other sites, so from this site you can explore to find other great book design sites, such as:

http://typophile.com/blog

http://www.typographyserved.com

Microsoft Help: online and offline

Your copy of Microsoft Word has help built into it (offline help — that you can launch when not connected to the internet). Press **F1** to open up the help in all versions of Word. Help files are tricky when tackling a new subject because you don't know what you're looking for, and help files tend to go off on confusing tangents. If you've given up on Word help previously, give it another go now that you've read this book and are consequently more knowledgeable (I hope).

Microsoft also supply valuable information with their online Office help. Currently this is called 'Office Help and How-To', and as I write these words in October 2013 covers versions 2007, 2010, 2011(Mac) and 2013. In fact, if you search around from Office Support, you can still find Word 2003 help.

http://office.microsoft.com/en-us/support/

eBook formatting

Amazon provides a lot of guidance on their Kindle Direct Publishing site. Click on the Community item on the top of the screen to visit the active user forums.

https://kdp.amazon.com/self-publishing/help

Amazon also have a free book (in Kindle format) about how to build a book for Kindle. It's called *Building Your Book for Kindle*. This covers how to build a book without straying far from Microsoft Word. There are plenty of things you can't do well with this approach, but it covers the basics, and if in book layout terms, you write simple fiction, then this could be all you need to make your Kindle book, at least to start with. In preparation for writing this *Format Your Book for Createspace: 2nd Edition*, I read many other books, looking for an intermediate guide to fit between Amazon's *Building Your Book for Kindle* (beginner level) and Paul Salvette's *The eBook Design and Development Guide* (advanced). Unfortunately I couldn't find a single book I was prepared to endorse. If you look for an intermediate book yourself, don't believe everything you read; I suggest you try several books to get different opinions.

Smashwords provides a free book about how to format a book for Smashwords called the *Smashwords Style Guide*. It's available in several languages. Much of the guidance is appropriate for KDP and other eBook publishing platforms.

http://www.smashwords.com/b/52

Helen Hanson is a writer who also gives advice on coding Kindle, ePub and formatting Createspace books. Here is her landing page for Kindle advice.

http://www.helenhanson.com/?p=892

Kindle Boards is a great forum for Kindle writers and readers. There's a forum called *Writers' Café*, which is great for asking questions about Kindle formatting. I'm on there as 'Tim C Taylor'. You can send private messages, so come on over and say, 'hi'.

http://www.kindleboards.com/

Liz Castro is an expert at CSS, ePUB coding, and a tool called InDesign, which is a desktop publishing tool. I've read and used her book *Straight to the Point* about coding ePUB format eBooks. Although it spends more time with InDesign than Microsoft Word, it is still well worth a look if you want to take your eBook formatting onto an advanced level.

http://www.elizabethcastro.com/epub/

Calibre is a free tool written by Kovid Goyal. It is aimed at readers, helping them to organize their libraries of eBooks. In practice, many writers use the Calibre conversion tools to generate their eBooks. You can save your Word document as type filtered html and use Calibre to convert this to a variety of eBook formats (selecting ZIP as your input format). Kovid knows what he is doing, and often pops up to explain things on another great site, MobileRead.com. Inevitably, Calibre doesn't always guess correctly what you want to do. It is highly configurable, but that can be more complicated than hand coding. Definitely worth a look, though. http://calibre-ebook.com/

Paul Salvette – has produced the best book I've seen so far on how to build eBooks: *The eBook Design and Development Guide* (available as a Kindle book). I don't quite agree with everything but it's close to how I build my own eBooks. This contains fairly advanced techniques and you will need to put in a little work if you're new to html and css coding. http://www.paulsalvette.com/

Indie Writers Unite — there are many forums and other groups where self-publishers and writers get together. My favorite is a Facebook Group called Indie Writers Unite. It's a place for people like us to hang out and help each other out, and formatting and publishing is certainly on the agenda. I'm on this group myself. I hope to meet you there.

http://www.facebook.com/groups/indiewriters/

About Tim C. Taylor

Tim C. Taylor lives with his family in an old village in England called Bromham. When he was a young and impressionable lad, between 1977 and 1978, several important things happened to him all at once: 2000AD, Star Wars, Blake's 7, and Dungeons & Dragons. Consequently, he now writes science fiction.

Tim's short fiction has been published in a number of magazines, and most recently in *Shoes, Ships & Cadavers* and *Further Conflicts*, anthologies that featured classy authors such as Alan Moore, Lauren Beukes, and Dan Abnett. His ambition is that one day, Moore, Beukes, and Abnett will proudly write in their bios that they once shared an anthology with Tim C. Taylor.

It wasn't always that way. Before a series of Doctor Who novels inspired him to start writing fiction in 2002, Tim wrote first music and then software. After twenty years in the software industry, Tim took a break in 2011, setting up Greyhart Press, a publisher of science fiction, horror, and fantasy. He also provides a range of formatting and editing services and has produced 150 eBooks and 40 paperbacks. He has been privileged to work on the fiction of some of his favorite authors, including Neil Gaiman, Lauren Beukes, Stephen Baxter, Ian Watson, Tanith Lee, Liz Williams... the list keeps growing!

While most of his time has been spent publishing or building books for other authors, Tim found time to complete his first two novels, a series called *The*

Reality War, published in February 2012. There are YA fantasy stories sitting on the shelf, and a military SF series underway.

In the real world, he is husband, Dad, sometime-brewer, and oftentimes-builder of Lego constructs to his son's designs. His favorite beer is *Uplift Ale*, named in honor of SF author David Brin, and available exclusively from his garage.

He has been using Microsoft Word ever since the days when it was only available for the Apple Mac, and the most powerful computer Apple had yet made was in fact their laser printer.

Find him on the web at www.timctaylor.com or on Twitter @TimCTaylor

APPENDIX A — HOW *THIS* BOOK WAS FORMATTED

I've asserted from the start that you can produce good print books from manuscripts typeset in nothing more than Microsoft Word... unless you need to work with images.

In writing and laying out the second edition of this book, I used Microsoft Word 2010 and 2013. The screenshots were captured at 96dpi, and then manipulated using a combination of Paint.NET and Adobe Photoshop CS6. The final PDF was produced using Adobe Acrobat Pro XI.

To create the eBook versions, I tagged formatting in the Word document (for example, I used Word's FIND and REPLACE to bracket each use of italics with <i> tags) and then copied and pasted into NotePad++ to tune up the html. Then I loaded into Sigil for more styling and tidying before compiling the Kindle version using Kindlegen.

Styles

I changed to my Createspace style set that I've created myself and saved. I then tweaked the paragraph spacing and set body text to Palatino Linotype 9.5pt, with lines set to *at least* 12pt, and with a 4pt spacing between paragraphs. I set hyperlinks by default to 8pt to prevent them interrupting the text so much. Headings are Franklin Gothic typeface.

Images

All images had to be 300dpi minimum. I used Paint.NET or Photoshop to enlarge and resample. In most cases I sharpened the image. In Photoshop, that came from the basic sharpen filter, and in Paint.NET, this is **Effects | Photo | Sharpen...** with a setting of 3-5.

With a little more space to play with in the printed version than the eBook, I added captions to most of the images. The main purpose was to enable a Table of Figures at the front so readers can zoom straight to the screenshot they want. I did this using Word's **Insert Caption** and **Table of Figures** buttons on the Ribbon.

References

Page number references to other pages in the book were inserted as field codes using Word's Cross-reference tool (in the REFERENCES part of the Ribbon). In order to set up the cross-reference, the target I pointed to needed to be either in heading style or occasionally a bookmark. Since I shifted the content around, this was far better than simply typing in the page numbers. All I had to do was select the entire document (CTRL+A) and press F9, and all the cross-reference page numbers were automatically updated.

One of the delights of non-fiction eBooks are active hyperlinks and other navigational tools that let you quickly access the topic you want, whether inside the book or outside on the internet. So for the eBook I converted all the cross-references to hyperlinks. This was a lot of work but worth it.

That's it!

If you have any questions, get in touch via my website (www.timctaylor.com).

If not, then what are you waiting for? Go make your book!

Good luck.

Tim C. Taylor, Bromham — October 2013